T0113320

Urgent Times

Other books in the NEW DEMOCRACY FORUM series:

The New Inequality: Creating Solutions for Poor America,
    by Richard B. Freeman

Reflecting All of Us: The Case for Proportional Representation,
    by Robert Richie and Steven Hall

*A Community of Equals: The Constitutional Protection of New
    Americans,* by Owen Fiss

Money and Politics: Financing Our Elections Democratically,
    by David Donnelly, Janice Fine, and Ellen S. Miller

Metro Futures: Economic Solutions for Cities and Their Suburbs,
    by Daniel D. Luria and Joel Rogers

Urgent Times

POLICING AND RIGHTS IN INNER-CITY COMMUNITIES

Tracey L. Meares
and Dan M. Kahan

Foreword by Eugene F. Rivers, 3d

Edited by Joshua Cohen and Joel Rogers
for *Boston Review*

BEACON PRESS
BOSTON

BEACON PRESS
25 Beacon Street
Boston, Massachusetts 02108-2892
www.beacon.org

Beacon Press books
are published under the auspices of
the Unitarian Universalist Association of Congregations.

05 04 03 02 01 00 99   8 7 6 5 4 3 2 1

This book is printed on recycled acid-free paper that contains at least 20
percent postconsumer waste and meets the uncoated paper ANSI/NISO
specifications for permanence as revised in 1992.

Text design by Christopher Kuntze
Composition by Wilsted & Taylor Publishing Services

Library of Congress Cataloging-in-Publication Data

Meares, Tracey L.
    Urgent times : policing and rights in inner-city communities /
Tracey L. Meares and Dan M. Kahan.
        p.   cm. — (New democracy forum)
    ISBN 0-8070-0605-x (pa)
    1. Community policing—United States.   2. Criminal justice,
Administration of—United States.   3. Law enforcement—
United States.   4. Civil rights—United States.   I. Kahan, Dan M.
II. Title.   III. Series.
HV7936.C83M42   1999
363.2'3'0973—dc21   99-23658

Contents

Foreword by Eugene F. Rivers, 3d / vii

Editors' Preface by Joshua Cohen
and Joel Rogers / xv

I

TRACEY L. MEARES AND DAN M. KAHAN
When Rights Are Wrong: The Paradox of
Unwanted Rights / 3

II

ALAN M. DERSHOWITZ
Rights and Interests / 33

JEAN BETHKE ELSHTAIN
Getting It Right / 40

JOEL F. HANDLER
It's Not So Simple / 45

CAROL S. STEIKER
More Wrong Than Rights / 49

WESLEY G. SKOGAN
Everybody's Business / 58

MARGARET A. BURNHAM
Twice Victimized / 63

FRANKLIN E. ZIMRING
A Multi-Problem Theory / 70

JEREMY WALDRON
Inalienable Rights / 76

BERNARD E. HARCOURT
Matrioshka Dolls / 81

ANTHONY PAUL FARLEY
Faith, Hope, and Charity / 89

RICHARD H. PILDES
The New Progressives / 93

III

TRACEY L. MEARES AND DAN M. KAHAN
Reply / 101

Notes / 112
About the Contributors / 116

Foreword

EUGENE F. RIVERS, 3d

*I*n the late 1980s, I moved to the Four Corners neigh-borhood in Dorchester. The community, one of Boston's poorest, was devastated by unemployment, drugs, crime, and guns. Families, schools, and churches were falling apart. And the people living there were suffering from a sense of futility, hopelessness, and spiritual death.

I went to Four Corners as minister of a faith commu-nity whose members were fired by a common mission. We would build a church, work the streets instead of the corporate boardrooms and suburban parlors, close the crack houses, bring jobs in, get guns out, keep people from killing each other, create some autonomous black institutions, restore faith and hope, and renew confi-dence in the great promise of all God's children.

With all these big ambitions, we had to start simply, and the place to begin was *personal safety*. The neighbor-hood was in a state of war, and Thomas Hobbes had it right about that state: "In such condition there is no place for industry, because the fruit thereof is uncertain, . . . no commodious building, no instruments of moving and removing such things as require much force, no knowledge of the face of the earth, no account of time, no arts, no letters, no society, and which is worst of all, continual fear and danger of violent death, and the life of man, solitary, poor, nasty, brutish, and short." People in our community had to be able to walk down the street without getting mugged, stabbed, or shot. If we couldn't deliver basic personal security, we couldn't do any of the fancy "arts, letters, and society" stuff. Kids don't want to go to school when they might get stabbed; adults don't want to invest their money, create jobs, or build homes when people are killing each other for drugs, leather jackets, sneakers, and gold chains.

When I moved to Four Corners, I had very little use for cops, and saw them as one of the main obstacles to public safety. The cops I knew—from Philadelphia, New Haven, and Boston—were basically white, racist, and sadistic. They would rob drug dealers of their drugs and money, and then arrest them for possession with intent to distribute, assault and battery against an officer, and resisting arrest. They would bust open the faces of Leroy and Rahim, throw them in jail, and charge them with defacing public property by staining police uniforms with their blood.

With the cops on the wrong side of the fight, we had to do the work of public safety ourselves. So the plan was to get kids back in church and teach them some elementary morality and respect for other people and for themselves (as well as some simple manners); patrol the streets and make sure that the gang-bangers and drug dealers weren't shooting people and selling poison; and put civilian review boards in place to watch the cops and keep them from getting in the way or doing serious human damage. We took the old-fashioned Black Panther idea of getting power back in the community, mixed in some honest religion instead of pop Marxism, and dropped the macho-armed-vanguard-of-the-people's-revolution nonsense.

We made real progress, one soul at a time, but also learned some hard lessons. Our big problem was that lots of the gang-bangers and drug dealers were smart and vicious: They had turf to protect, and they were not going to back off, lie down, or hold hands and drop to their knees to praise the Lord with Reverend Rivers. They were shooting through our walls and windows (they shot up my house twice), threatening our kids, killing each other, and selling dope. Same old story: If we couldn't keep the peace on the streets, then we couldn't do much else.

At this point, we tried something really different. Unlike lots of our political allies, we decided to be rational and learn something, instead of being ideologically pure and dumb. We figured out that we couldn't keep the peace on the streets without the cops. That meant that we needed to get past the 1960s idea of civilian review boards that watch over the police, and start figuring out how to cooperate with them. We had to take *joint responsibility* for the streets, not just punish racist cops.

So we built a larger coalition of churches around the

model of using faith communities to fight violence (the Ten-Point Coalition) and developed some creative ways of collaborating with the cops. To develop the agenda for the Coalition and collaboration, I talked to the young drug dealers in the neighborhood—they were the ones who knew what needed to be done. We haven't stopped patrolling our neighborhoods; we know where the trouble is, and can help stop it before it starts. But we also have a working relationship with the cops in our area. When there's trouble, we direct them to the source. If some punk is selling drugs on the street, we know how to get the street cleaned. When Rahim doesn't get himself straight, we tell him that Officer O'Connor will be visiting him in a dark alley. And for more than a year now, we have met every week with cops, probation officers, and social workers to talk about how to keep the Boston Bloods and Crips in line. We know who they are, what they are doing wrong, what they are buying and selling, and how to get to them. The result is that the Bloods and Crips are quiet. Because we know who's been making trouble, the cops want to cooperate with us.

It is a strategic relationship, based on an exchange, not on love or friendship—we have information and an organization on the streets; they have power and know how to deal with the talentless tenth. And now the streets are a lot safer. That's community policing, Boston style.

Which brings me to the topic of this important book

in the *New Democracy Forum* series. For starters, let's get one thing clear: Tracey Meares and Dan Kahan have performed a great public service. Whoever is right on the details—whether Meares and Kahan, or Dershowitz, Burnham, Steiker, and the other critics—the powerful argument in the lead essay has opened up a major debate on a promising idea about how to keep streets safe without throwing out essential legal safeguards. If you live where I live, you know that's a life-and-death issue. And you also know that community policing is better than throwing people in jail: It is more democratic, more humane, and less costly (all that construction money being thrown at new prisons could be used on teachers and schools). I am sure that the arguments here, pro and con, will not settle the constitutional issues, but they jumpstart the debate.

Part of the argument in the book is about why courts decided to impose more restrictions on cops in the 1960s: Meares and Kahan think the courts were trying to protect black people from racist cops because they did not trust the democratic process to provide the protections. Dershowitz and others think the courts finally got smart about the dangers that unbridled cops present to everyone, black or white—that the protections were about preventing the abuse of discretionary power, not about racism.

I am not a historian or a lawyer, and I don't claim to know the right answer, but the historical argument is not where the real action is, anyway. The big issue is what should happen now. If people in a neighborhood want to have a stronger police presence and cut the cops more slack, should the courts get in the way? If the residents who show up at a public meeting want to let the cops randomly search all the houses in the neighborhood—even if it means that their own house will be among the targets—should judges play "father knows best"?

It is a hard issue and, from my experience on the streets, I know both sides of the argument. I have ministered to kids who have been beaten up by racist cops, so throwing more discretion to cops doesn't do a lot for me. But I also know that we can't keep the peace on the streets just by tying the cops' hands.

Which side is right? Wrong question. The basic idea of community policing is that we need more cooperation between cops and residents of communities, especially high-crime communities; the starting point is that the cops have to be ready to work with the community, and the community has to establish a zero-tolerance policy toward mayhem. But let's face it: We haven't yet figured out the best ways to work together. We know how to give cops discretion and turn them loose; we know how to tie their hands with endless lists of rules. What we don't know yet is the best way to *guide* their discretion so that they don't have to search every apartment in the building to figure out who has been running dope, or every house on the block to know where the guns are. People in the neighborhood who take joint responsibility for public safety already know that. To provide guided discretion, we need to experiment with different ways of building cooperation between communities, who have this kind of essential information, and cops, who know what to do with it.

I don't want the cops turned loose without anyone watching—they can't be trusted, and wouldn't know what to do, anyway. But I also don't want someone looking over their shoulder every time they make a move. We need to learn how to strike the right balance. Learning is an issue for life, not law. The lawyers have helped us all by starting the debate. Now let the real experimentation begin.

Editors' Preface

JOSHUA COHEN AND JOEL ROGERS

The New Democracy Forum aims to foster honest, serious discussion of pressing national problems and constructive debate about political solutions to them. Crime, particularly crime in our central cities, has dominated state and local politics for more than a generation. The most common policy response has been to build more prisons, with the result that our rate of incarceration is now second only to Russia's. But there has also been some recent innovation in policing strategies. The most important of these, generically described as "community policing," combines greater police/community cooperation with increased police discretion. Cooperation gives community policing a democratic aura, and it may be helping to push down crime rates in cities that are experimenting with it. Granting increased discretionary powers to the police, however, prompts fears about the violation of individual rights.

The problem is particularly difficult in communities with high crime rates, where lots of people want more discretion for the police. This preference puts them on a collision course with the body of law developed by the Supreme Court (especially in the 1960s) that greatly strengthened individual protections in the area of criminal procedure. Thus far, the courts have been reluctant to roll back these rights, even at the behest of embattled communities.

These disputes—about courts and democracy, rights and crime—are the focus of the lead essay for this volume in the New Democracy Forum Series, by University of Chicago law professors Tracey Meares and Dan Kahan. They argue that the criminal procedure protections developed in the 1960s were largely a response to concerns about racism, but that those concerns have now abated. Central-city communities should therefore be awarded a larger role in determining their own "balance of order and liberty" without constant judicial second-guessing.

The Meares/Kahan argument is highly controversial, as the responses here demonstrate. Some critics argue that the changes in criminal procedure made in the 1960s were not driven by concerns about racism, but by long-standing fears about the abuse of state power. Others question the thought that racism has diminished so much that the courts can step back and simply let normal democratic processes monitor the police. And some think that crime-ridden communities are not freely choosing to give the police greater discretion, but are act-ing out of desperation. No one thinks that greater police discretion, even if "authorized" by the community, is a cause for public celebration. The hard issue is whether there is a better and more democratic solution to the problem of urban crime.

I

When Rights Are Wrong
The Paradox of Unwanted Rights

TRACEY L. MEARES AND DAN M. KAHAN

Many tenants within CHA housing, apparently convinced by sad experience that the larger community will not provide normal law enforcement services to them, are prepared to forgo their own constitutional rights. They apparently want this court to suspend their neighbors' rights as well. . . . This Court has faith that parents and grandparents living in and around CHA housing will reclaim their families and restore to their children self-respect and respect for other human beings. If they do, government efforts will succeed; if they do not, all efforts of government, whether within or without constitutional restraints, will fail.

—Judge Wayne Anderson, granting a motion
to enjoin mass searches of public housing

I understand the right to privacy, but when my baby can't play outside and your baby can't go to school without being shot and killed, what about their *rights?*

—Alverta Munlyn, resident of public housing

*T*hanks to the American Civil Liberties Union and a federal district court judge, residents of Chicago's low-income housing projects currently have the right to be free from mass building searches. The ACLU challenged the legality of such searches in a class action lawsuit filed on the residents' behalf, and Judge Wayne Anderson agreed that the building searches violated the residents' constitutional rights.

The decision sounds like the rare case of a judge protecting a vulnerable population from police coercion, but for one important detail: an overwhelming majority of the residents *opposed* the ACLU's effort to block the building searches. The Chicago Housing Authority (CHA) adopted its building search policy as an emergency response to the deadly outbursts of gunfire associated with incessant gang warfare; in one four-day period near this time, the police recorded more than three hundred gunfire incidents in the Robert Taylor Homes and Stateway Gardens projects. When the ACLU filed suit, the elected representatives of eighteen of CHA's nineteen projects intervened to support the CHA.[1] But Judge Anderson dismissed the residents' willingness to consent to building searches as evidence of the corrosive effect of poverty and crime on their own "self-respect."

Judge Anderson's ruling was certainly paradoxical. We ordinarily think of rights as belonging to individuals. Rights express the respect owed to each of us as autonomous actors whose choices about how to secure our own well-being shouldn't be second-guessed by political officials. Yet in the CHA case, Judge Anderson invoked the residents' rights in order to *overrule* their choices on the grounds that he knew better than they what policies treated them with respect.

As strange as this story seems, it is no aberration. The Chicago Housing Authority's building searches represent only one of many law enforcement policies attacked by civil libertarians and invalidated by the courts on the grounds that they violate the rights of the very individuals who support them. Before it derailed the CHA's building searches, for example, the ACLU sued to block the installation of metal detectors requested by project residents. It has also attacked youth curfews and "gang-loitering" provisions on the grounds that these policies promote the harassment of inner-city residents—even though residents of the inner city have in fact been the driving political force behind many of these measures.

The problems posed by inner-city crime defy easy solutions. Reasonable people can—and often do—disagree on whether building searches, curfews, anti-loitering ordinances, and the like work at all, and, more pointedly, on whether they will work well enough to justify the burdens they impose on individual liberty. What is unreasonable, however, is to assume that the individuals most intimately affected by these policies are not smart enough or are not informed enough or do not value liberty enough to decide these issues for themselves.

Why do some civil libertarians and courts feel constrained to override the freedom of these persons in the name of respecting their rights? The answer is that they subscribe to an anachronistic and unduly abstract understanding of individual rights—one fashioned to address political conditions that, by and large, no longer characterize American society. Contemporary political conditions require a new conception of rights—one that assures that the difficult choices surrounding building searches, curfews, anti-loitering provisions, and the like are made by the people who have the biggest stake in them.

RIGHTS, 1960s STYLE

Rights have histories. They are fashioned in a particular social and political context for the purpose of achieving particular ends. The prevailing understanding of rights in American criminal law was fashioned in the 1960s, as a response to the problem of institutionalized racism.

As is well known, in the decades between the post-Reconstruction years and the civil rights movement, African-Americans were excluded from meaningful participation in American political life. The South used a host of techniques—poll taxes, literacy tests, malapportionment, and outright physical intimidation—to deny African-Americans a voice in electoral politics. Things were little better in the North, where machine politics of the kind made famous by the elder Richard Daley in Chicago effectively excluded legally enfranchised African-Americans and other minorities from meaningful influence on the political process in America's inner cities.

Law enforcement institutions played a vital role in reinforcing American apartheid. The horrific television images of blacks in Birmingham, including children, being attacked by police dogs, and of police officers wielding clubs and high-pressure water hoses are indelible and poignant reminders of the South's violent resistance to civil rights progress. But Northern urban minorities were also frequently subject to violent abuse. In the late 1960s, for example, Chicago police led the nation in the slaying of private citizens, who were euphemistically characterized as "fleeing felons" to mask the routine use of excessive force by police against racial minorities. The police also exploited seemingly benign offense categories, such as disorderly conduct, vagrancy, and loitering, to bully minority youths and adults who had the audacity to challenge police authority.

Excluded from politics and harassed by police, African-Americans were also denied adequate police protection. In the mid-1960s, African-Americans were an especially vulnerable population: they comprised more than half of the known homicide victims and were nearly twice as likely as whites to be the victims of robbery, rape, aggravated assault, burglary, and auto theft.

How did police respond to these problems? They didn't. Throughout the country, the criminal justice system paid much less attention to violent crimes committed against members of minority groups than to those committed against whites. In addition, the police systematically disregarded more common "disorder" offenses in minority communities, dismissing prostitution, public drinking, gambling, and even simple assaults as "typically Negro." This toleration of crime and disorder helped to accelerate urban decay, driving critical commercial establishments, as well as working-class residents with the resources to leave, out of poor inner-city neighborhoods.

Against this background, the Warren Court fashioned its well-known array of procedural rights in criminal law. From the *Miranda* rule to detailed search-and-seizure guidelines, to the "void for vagueness" doctrine (used to invalidate vague regulations on the grounds that they leave too much room for abuse), these guarantees were animated by two principles—"community distrust" and "discretion skepticism"—that together can be characterized as the 1960s conception of rights. To be sure, this conception is often presented in very abstract terms, as if it descended directly from first principles of political theory and as if anyone who believes in rights at all must embrace it. But the 1960s conception is best understood contextually, as a program to counteract the distorting influence of institutionalized racism on America's criminal justice system and, more generally, on American democracy.[2]

The 1960s conception of rights showed distrust for communities insofar as it licensed relentless judicial second-guessing of judgments about the appropriate balance between order and liberty arrived at through normal democratic processes. Of course, all rights reflect some degree of community distrust because they protect the interests of vulnerable minorities from majority overreaching. What made the 1960s conception of rights uniquely "distrustful" was its extension of searching judicial scrutiny to basic neighborhood policing techniques that historically had been viewed as important to promoting the welfare of the community at large.

Institutionalized racism fully justified this wariness about familiar techniques and about the capacity of normal democratic politics to protect citizens from police abuse. However widely it may have been felt previously, the coercive impact of neighborhood policing practices was by the 1960s obviously concentrated upon African-Americans, who by virtue of their exclusion from the political process had little or no say about the justness or appropriateness of particular law enforcement practices, and little or no recourse when standard procedures were abused. Under these circumstances, majority approval did not signal that the individuals most affected by an invasive procedure or law viewed its impact on liberty as justified by its contribution to order. That's what searching judicial review was meant to guarantee: by expanding individual rights against the prerogatives of the police, it would correct for the failure of the democratic process to take into account the views and interests of African-Americans.

In a famous 1960 *Yale Law Journal* article, "Vagrancy and Arrest on Suspicion," Justice William O. Douglas leveled exactly this critique against anti-loitering laws, then a staple of American policing. It was naive to defer to the majority's approval of vagrancy and loitering laws, Douglas asserted, because those arrested under such laws typically came from minority groups with insufficient political clout to "protect themselves," and without "the prestige to prevent an easy laying-on of hands by the police." Douglas later authored the Court's opinion in *Papachristou v. Jacksonville*, which invalidated anti-loitering laws as unconstitutionally "vague."

Papachristou embodies the "discretion skepticism" characteristic of the 1960s conception of rights. In this decision, and others like it, the Supreme Court insisted that the authority of law enforcement officials to arrest and search individuals be defined with exacting precision.

This jurisprudential innovation, too, was motivated by anxiety about institutionalized racism and associated with corresponding failures of democracy. While allowing for "discretion" in policing advances the public interest by giving law enforcers the flexibility to respond to circumstances too numerous and diverse to be addressed in detail by legislative rulemakers, it also threatens the public good by giving law enforcers the latitude to abuse their power for personal ends. The primary check against such abuse is the accountability of law enforcers to the community's political representatives. In the political context of the 1960s, however, law enforcement officials were accountable only to representatives of the white majority. Predictably and for precisely this reason, the police often used their discretion to harass and repress minorities.

Insisting that law enforcement authority be exercised according to hyper-precise rules was a device for impeding the tendency of law enforcers to accommodate the demands of racist white political establishments. Such rules also made it much easier for courts to detect and punish racially motivated abuses of authority. Impeding political responsiveness is not always a good thing, but under the circumstances an expanded set of rights was a necessary corrective for the failure of the democratic process to represent the interests of all citizens and to monitor abuses of power.

THE 1990s WORLD

Given its historical context—the nature of the problems that then confronted African-Americans, and the Court's own institutional capacities—the 1960s conception of rights deserves admiration. The same cannot necessarily be said, however, about its continued enforcement, for the 1990s present a dramatically different set of social and political conditions.

To begin with, African-Americans are no longer excluded from the nation's democratic political life. Voter registration levels among African-Americans skyrocketed almost immediately after the enactment of the Voting Rights Act, and in all regions of the country, African-Americans have translated the power of their votes into political representation. Never higher than 3 percent before 1970, the size of the African-American contingent in Congress grew to 9 percent by the mid 1990s—close to the proportion of African-Americans in the population. Between 1970 and 1983, the number of black representatives to state governments doubled. The number of African-American mayors increased more than fivefold during the same period, and the number of city council members quadrupled. During the 1980s and 1990s, many of America's largest cities—including New York, Los Angeles, Chicago, and San Francisco—have been run by African-American mayors.

Growth in African-American political strength has also changed the face of urban police forces nationwide. In Chicago, 25 percent of police officers are African-American; in Washington, D.C., a majority are. New York City, Washington, D.C., and Los Angeles have all employed African-American police chiefs. It's no longer plausible for courts to simply assume a deeply antagonistic relationship between the police and minorities, or that the democratic process is still so dominated by racial exclusion that the court must substitute for it as monitors of police practice.

Crime in minority communities has also changed dramatically since the 1960s: it has grown substantially worse. While national crime rates have been steadily declining during the past decade, they have been increasing in the predominantly minority neighborhoods of America's inner cities. Because most crime is intraracial, disproportionate victimization of minorities goes hand in hand with the involvement of minorities in the criminal justice system. Fully one-third of African-American men between the ages of twenty and twenty-nine are currently incarcerated, on probation, or on parole.

Moreover, the high proportion of African-American men who have been convicted of a crime is a cause, as well as a consequence, of the inner-city crime problem. As more persons are convicted of crime, less stigma is attached to law-breaking. The higher the number of men incarcerated, the greater the number of single mothers, whose own economic struggles deprive them of the time needed to shield their children from the pressures that draw young people into crime. The perception that African-American men are disproportionately involved in crime breeds distrust and suspicion of all African-American men, putting even law-abiding citizens at a disadvantage in the employment market and eroding the neighborly bonds essential to community self-policing.

In short, crime enfeebles social structures, enfeebled social structures produce more crime, and crime destroys

African-Americans' wealth and security. This self-reinforcing dynamic constitutes one of the largest impediments to improving the economic and social standing of African-Americans today.

How well does the 1960s conception of rights fit the political reality of the 1990s? In a word, horribly.

To begin with, community distrust and discretion skepticism address problems that no longer dominate American political life. Only someone who fails to read the newspapers could think that racially motivated police brutality is a thing of the past, but only someone who reads the papers with astonishing selectivity could believe that the problem of police racism today is indistinguishable from what it was thirty years ago. In 1968, Frank Rizzo emerged as a national political figure by orchestrating racial terrorism as police commissioner (and later mayor) of Philadelphia. By 1999, ambitious urban mayors like Richard Daley were making a point of energetically criticizing racist cops; urban police chiefs who oversaw racist forces, such as Daryl Gates, were finding themselves unceremoniously forced out of their jobs and relegated to the cultural and political fringe.

This welcome change is a consequence of decisive reforms secured by the civil rights revolution. Exercising the powers secured to their constituents by the Voting Rights Act, African-American political leaders have demanded and obtained more effective bureaucratic procedures for punishing police brutality.

These procedures do not completely eliminate the risk of harassment associated with aggressive "order-maintenance" policing. But given the opportunities that African-Americans now have to protect themselves from state abuse through politics, it's perfectly reasonable for them to believe, as Harvard's Randall Kennedy has written, that "the principal injury suffered by African-Americans in relation to criminal matters is not over-enforcement but under-enforcement of the laws."[3]

Ironically, the 1960s conception of rights now poses a significant impediment to vanquishing this particular legacy of racism. Reduction of crime is one of the primary purposes to which minority communities are putting their new-found political power. Instead of shunning the police, inner-city residents are demanding that police give them the protection they have historically been denied. Yet professed civil libertarians—including the ACLU—have repeatedly invoked the 1960s conception of rights to block efforts by inner-city residents to liberate themselves from the destructive effects of crime.

The invalidation of the Chicago Housing Authority's building search policy is one striking example of the mismatch between the 1960s conception of rights and the political realities of the 1990s; another is the invalidation of Chicago's "gang-loitering" ordinance. Enacted in 1992, this law was designed to restrict the congregation of known gang members on street corners and other public ways. The ACLU attacked the ordinance as a throwback to the pre-*Papachristou* era, when police officers used vague loitering ordinances to intimidate and harass racial minorities. A state court agreed, in a decision recently affirmed by the U.S. Supreme Court,[4] describing the ordinance as an exercise of power reminiscent of a police state.

The picture of Chicago's gang-loitering ordinance that the ACLU and the court painted is simply false. The law was not enacted to oppress the city's minority residents; rather it sprang from the grievances of these very citizens, who demanded effective action to rid their neighborhoods of drive-by shootings, fighting, and open-air drug dealing. The ordinance was passed by an overwhelming margin in the Chicago City Council, with key support from aldermen representing the city's most impoverished, crime-ridden districts, whose residents are predominantly members of racial and ethnic minorities.

The claim that the ordinance invited arbitrary or discriminatory enforcement was also unfounded. In fact, the ordinance was accompanied by carefully considered guidelines. For example, only a small number of officers in each police district were permitted to enforce the ordinance. They could do so, moreover, only in specified areas of a district, areas with demonstrated gang activity. Before specifying enforcement "hot spots," district commanders were to consult with community residents.

What's more, it appears that the ordinance succeeded in decreasing crime before the courts intervened. Police data indicate that aggressive enforcement of the ordinance had led to substantial decreases in gang- and narcotics-related homicides and aggravated batteries in the districts with the most serious problems. Blocking the policies makes law enforcement protection less effective while adding no new political checks against law enforcement abuses.

Another effective law enforcement policy that has fallen victim to the 1960s conception of rights is the youth curfew. More than half of the major cities in the United States have enacted curfew legislation since 1990. They have been fought every step of the way by civil libertarians who argue that curfews interfere with the choices of individual teens and their parents, and invite racially motivated harassment by the police. Some courts, though not all, agree.

But again, the civil libertarian critique defies political reality. African-Americans, far from opposing curfews, have supplied much of the political energy behind their resurgence. Edna Pemberton—an African-American mother of ten who spearheaded the campaign for a Dallas curfew—described the charge that curfews fuel racial harassment as "an ACLU scare tactic that polarized the community." Even inner-city teens generally favor curfews. One poll showed that 70 percent of African-

American teens in Washington, D.C., supported that city's curfew.

The claim that curfews interfere with individual choice is naive. It overlooks the degree to which juveniles' decisions to participate in inner-city nightlife are constrained by unchosen and widely resented norms. Willingness to venture into the dangerous after-hours world can be seen as a sign of toughness among inner-city teens, and the reluctance to do so as a sign of weakness. Even youths who prefer not to participate in such behavior—and whose parents desperately prefer the same—can thus find themselves pressured to join in. Curfews help to extricate juveniles from these pressures.

Ironically, inner-city curfews are frequently opposed by residents of affluent, largely white, suburban communities. These suburbanites fear that curfews will be used against their children, who occasionally go into the city for entertainment and don't face the pressures that curfews are meant to counteract. The puzzle is why civil libertarians and the courts side with the suburbanites, who have much less at stake with regard to the crime problems of the inner city than do inner-city families.

Civil libertarians and courts offer several justifications for overriding the decisions of inner-city residents on these issues, none of them satisfying. One is that individuals choose building searches, curfews, gang-loitering ordinances, and the like only because society at large refuses to address the social inequities at the root of inner-city crime. It is true that society at large now refuses to address social inequities, and it is also true that residents of the inner city face unfairly truncated options—but what follows? That those residents should live with gangs, murder, and drugs until justice "rolls down like the waters"? That they should be made to accept the one option—rampant crime—that they prefer least and about which they might try to do something?

Another version of this argument is strategic: courts shouldn't let the residents of the inner city choose "quick-fix" law enforcement policies because this would reduce society's long-term incentive to remedy inequity. This claim is exceedingly dubious. Thirty years' worth of real-world experience belies the idea that spiraling inner-city crime will somehow force powerful interests *outside* the inner city to revitalize these communities. The only thing that can force such change is sustained community-level political organizing. That organizing is going on, and it is often just these organizers who argue in support of curfews, building searches, and gang-loitering ordinances.

But the real question for civil libertarians is this: Why can't we trust residents of the inner city to decide for themselves whether the strategic objection makes sense? Shouldn't these individuals be allowed to determine whether this is the most sensible way to improve *their* lives?

Civil libertarians have an answer to these questions, too: no. The judgment and "self-respect" of inner-city residents, they sometimes maintain, have been deformed by social deprivation. Consequently, they lack the capacity to make critical assessments of curfews, gang-loitering ordinances, building searches, and other similar policies.

This contention is rife with self-contradiction. Civil libertarians usually take immense pride in their resistance to paternalism. Respecting individual dignity, they maintain, requires society to refrain from forcing an idealized set of values and preferences on its citizens. Yet, upon the discovery that inner-city residents favor policies that the ACLU believes violate individual rights, too many civil libertarians resort to the very kind of paternalism they ought to abhor. The support given by inner-city residents for building searches, loitering ordinances, and curfews, they argue, should be ignored because it is a product of the debasing influences of crime and poverty. The appropriate way to show respect for these individuals is to enforce the rights they would value had they formed their preferences in a better environment. To treat them with dignity, society must—in the words of the notorious anti-liberal Jean-Jacques Rousseau—"force them to be free"!

But the civil libertarian claim that inner-city residents lack critical judgment is not just paradoxical—it is manifestly false. When the ACLU filed suit in the building-search case, CHA residents were vigorously debating the appropriateness of the policy. Although many residents supported the existing CHA policy on searches, many others advocated guidelines to restrict the searches to the hours immediately following a report of gunfire. The heated debate concerning the CHA building searches among CHA residents demonstrates that these individuals do not just accept rules uncritically. Rather, like other self-respecting persons in a tough situation, they reflect, they complain, they demand, they argue, they fight, and they ultimately *decide* what the best course of action is—unless, of course, the power of self-government is taken away from them.

Indeed, the worst consequence of the ongoing commitment to the 1960s conception of rights may be its *dis*empowering effect on inner-city communities. Criminologists have long recognized that inner-city crime both creates and is sustained by atomization and distrust, which in turn make it harder for individuals to engage in the cooperative self-policing characteristic of crime-free communities. A healthy democratic political life can help to repair these conditions. That is precisely what residents of the inner city enjoy when they are free to decide for themselves whether to adopt or approve building searches, gang-loitering ordinances, curfews, and the like. Thus, in addition to standing in the way of potentially effective law enforcement policies, the 1960s conception of rights preempts deliberative experiences

that reduce crime through their effect on public dispositions and habits.

RIGHTS, 1990S STYLE

What is to be done? Abandoning protections of individuals suspected or accused of criminal activity is obviously
not the answer. No one believes that such rights are unimportant. Moreover, it would be silly to argue that the
legacy and teachings of the 1960s conception of individual rights have no relevance today. At the same time, it is
equally clear that a rigid application of those views is no
longer appropriate. We need a new conception of these
rights, informed by premises that fit the unique political
conditions of the 1990s, including the emergent political
power of African-Americans in the inner cities and the
devastating effects of inner-city crime on the social and
economic prospects of African-Americans today.

In fact, the U.S. Supreme Court seems poised to over-
haul its jurisprudence. For technical reasons, the six-
Justice majority that invalidated the Chicago gang-
loitering ordinance had to confine its attention to the
text of law, and ignored the administrative safeguards
designed to ensure that police would enforce it only to
prevent intimidating displays of gang authority. But in a
crucial concurring opinion, Justices Sandra Day O'Connor and Stephen Breyer made it clear that they would
uphold a law that incorporated such safeguards in the

text. Presumably the three dissenters in the case would do the same.

In sum, a clear majority of Justices are ready to retool constitutional doctrine to accommodate the democratic revolution now taking place in inner-city policing. But how exactly should they do it?

A 1990s conception of rights should be informed by two principles: *community burden-sharing* and *guided discretion*. The first determines when courts should relax their individualist distrust of community judgments, while the second assures that the trust that will be extended to exercises of community power is not abused.

Let's start with burden-sharing. It's commonplace to describe constitutional rights—particularly those that relate to criminal justice—as guaranteeing a reasonable balance between liberty and order. "Burden-sharing," a principle associated primarily with the constitutional theory of John Hart Ely, helps courts to determine whether the balance struck by any particular policy is reasonable. If the coercive aspect of a particular policy is being visited on a powerless minority, the courts make an independent assessment of whether the benefits in terms of order outweigh the costs in terms of liberty. This explains why courts strictly scrutinize policies that discriminate on the basis of race, restrict "dangerous" speech, or impose special obligations on account of religion.

But when a community can be seen as sharing in the coercive burden of a particular policy, the courts are much less likely to second-guess political institutions on whether the trade-off between liberty and order is worthwhile. This explains the deference courts afford to generally applicable laws under a host of constitutional provisions, including the Privileges and Immunities Clause, the dormant Commerce Clause, and the Free Exercise Clause. When courts defer to the political process in these contexts, they are not saying that the majority gets to decide what rights minorities have, but rather that the willingness of the majority to bear a particular burden suggests that the policy in question doesn't embody the political undervaluation of liberty that "rights" are meant to prevent.

The broad 1960s conception of rights rested on a presumption that white communities never shared in the burdens imposed by law enforcement techniques that restricted the liberty of African-Americans because members of the white majority community could use their political power to protect themselves from discretionary coercion. That assumption made sense in the 1960s, given racism and the virtual disenfranchisement of African-Americans in the South.

But it makes a lot less sense today, given the political strength of African-Americans and their own legitimate concern to free themselves from the ravages of inner-city crime. So instead of viewing all law enforcement techniques with suspicion—adopting the strong presumption that the democratic process is unable to monitor the exercise of police power—courts should ask whether the community in question is participating in the burden that a particular law imposes on individual freedom. If it is, the courts should presume, as they do in myriad other settings, that the law does not violate individual rights.

Building searches easily pass the burden-sharing test. The burden of unannounced mass searches falls on everyone who lives in the projects, not just on persons suspected of wrongdoing. The political representatives of these individuals, moreover, have unambiguously expressed their support for the searches. To be sure, not *everyone* who lives in the projects approves of the trade-off between submitting to this intrusive law enforcement technique and the increased security it delivers. But such disagreement comes with the territory of democracy. Because the dissenting individuals have every chance to voice their opposition in the political process, and because there is every reason to believe that the majority—whose members were affected in exactly the same way—give due weight to the dissenters' interests, there is no good reason for courts to second-guess the community's determination that building searches strike a fair balance between liberty and order. Of course, reasonable people disagree about the proper way to strike that balance, but the role of democracy is to settle such disagreements. Unless the process itself is deficient, the courts should defer to those settlements.

Gang-loitering ordinances and curfews likewise pass the burden-sharing test, albeit in a less straightforward fashion. These laws do indeed burden the liberty of a minority within the community—gang members in the one case, and juveniles in the other—many of whom might be disenfranchised. But this minority is by no means a despised group whose legitimate interests are disregarded by the process. Inner-city teens and even gang members are linked to the majority within their communities by strong social and familial ties. It is precisely because the majority of inner-city residents care so deeply about their welfare that this majority favors relatively mild gang-loitering and curfew laws as alternatives to draconian penalties for gang-related crimes, severe mandatory minimum prison sentences for drug distribution, and similarly punitive measures, which inner-city residents view as intolerably destructive. The pervasive sense of linked fate between the majority of inner-city residents and the youths affected by curfews and loitering ordinances furnishes a compelling reason *not* to override the community's determination that such measures enhance rather than detract from liberty in their communities.

Indeed, there is a profound tension between individual liberty and judicial decisions striking down such laws. Many inner-city residents view gang-loitering ordinances and curfews as tolerable, *moderate* ways to steer youths away from criminality. They realize that when courts prohibit such crime prevention measures, legislatures compensate with longer prison terms for lawbreaking. If the police cannot order kids off the streets today, all too often they will end up taking them to jail tomorrow. The self-defeating result is a society that shows its respect for individual liberty by destroying ever greater amounts of it.

Now consider the principle of "guided discretion" in policing practice and procedures. The 1960s conception of rights insists on hyper-specific rules because it assumes that white political establishments can't be relied upon to punish law enforcers who abuse their discretionary powers in order to harass minorities. That anxiety is no longer so well founded: law enforcers in America's big cities are accountable to political establishments that more fairly represent African-Americans than they have done in the past. Uncompromising hostility to discretion is therefore inappropriate.

This doesn't mean that the law should regard such discretion as an unvarnished good. Even assuming political accountability, granting unbounded discretion to the police creates a risk that individual law enforcers will be able to disregard the will of the community without detection. It also creates the risk that officials will concentrate burdens on a powerless or despised segment of the community, thereby undermining the principle of community burden-sharing. Hyper-specific rules are unnecessary under the principle of guided discretion, but this principle does require communities to allocate authority in a manner that minimizes these risks.

Chicago's anti-gang loitering ordinance is a good example of a law enforcement policy that satisfies the guided discretion principle. The ordinance was implemented through regulations that clearly specified who counted as a "gang member," what kinds of behavior counted, which officers could enforce the law, and in what neighborhood areas it could be enforced. When evaluated against these regulations, misuse of the ordinance would have been easy to spot. Had these guidelines been written into the text of the law itself, the Supreme Court would likely have upheld the gang-loitering ordinance, whether or not it satisfied the demand for hyper-precision associated with the 1960s conception of rights.

The Chicago Housing Authority's building searches present a closer case. The policy involved little risk of selective enforcement precisely because it consisted of indiscriminate, mass searches. Nevertheless, the policy placed no limits on when such searches could be conducted. Indeed, officials sometimes failed to carry one out until several days after gunfire had been reported. As a result, nothing prevented use of the sweeps as a prophylactic rather than as an emergency measure. Thus the principle of guided discretion might have supported requiring the CHA to develop guidelines on the timing of building searches—a result that would have tightened the fit between this law enforcement technique and the desires of the residents. Judge Anderson, in contrast, ruled that even such guidelines wouldn't have solved the conflict between building searches and the residents' rights.

THE TYRANNY OF LEGAL ABSTRACTION

In his 1960 *Yale Law Journal* article, Justice Douglas complained that "a disproportionate part of the energies of [the legal] profession is devoted to the semantics of the law." He continued, "[T]he discourse with which we tend to preoccupy ourselves is pretty much in the pattern of theological discourse. The priests of the profession argue and debate about nice points of law that may seem important to those who lead smug lives in ivory towers but quite unimportant in the life of the nation." The specific targets of Douglas's fire were courts that had invoked colonial precedents to uphold anti-vagrancy laws.

Though civil libertarians view themselves as Douglas's heirs, they misperceive the forest of his critique for the trees. Douglas criticized vagrancy laws on the grounds that the legal abstractions used to defend them were out of keeping with contemporary circumstances—namely, the discriminatory enforcement of vagrancy laws against effectively disenfranchised minorities. But circumstances have changed since 1960. Today African-Americans exercise considerable political clout in our nation's inner cities, and far from being terrorized by anti-loitering laws, curfews, and building searches, many inner-city residents *support* these measures as potent weapons against the crime that drastically diminishes their economic and social prospects.

The courts and civil libertarians who invoke the outmoded 1960s conception of rights are now the ones guilty of reducing law to a "theological discourse" divorced from "the life of the nation." Such scholasticism, moreover, has very real and painful consequences. Defenders of liberty can do much better.

❧ II ❧

Rights and Interests

ALAN M. DERSHOWITZ

*P*rofessors Meares and Kahan present a parochial, Afrocentric view of rights, which reminds me of the question my grandmother used to ask when I would joyously tell her that the Brooklyn Dodgers had won the pennant: "Is that good or bad for the Jews?" Meares and Kahan seem to judge every application of legal rights by whether it is good or bad for the majority of inner-city blacks in the 1990s. But rights are not, as Justice Jackson once reminded us, like a limited railroad ticket, good for this train at this day only: they are designed for all people and for an enduring period of time.

The Meares/Kahan essay begins with an historical error. The rights about which they speak did not grow exclusively out of an effort to remedy institutionalized racism. Rights do have histories, and the right of every American to be secure against unlawful police intrusion grew out of a long history of governmental abuse against disempowered people of all backgrounds. The 1960s followed on the heels of McCarthyism and earlier anti-immigrant and nativist abuses. Moreover, there was no revolution of *rights* with regard to police practices in the

1960s. The real revolution of the 1960s involved *remedies*. The rights had long been established in principle but were being ignored in practice. By enforcing these old rights with new remedies—particularly exclusionary rules and required warnings applicable to state as well as federal cases—the courts fulfilled earlier promises. Even then, the majority of blacks, like the majority of whites, did not agree that guilty defendants should go free because their rights had been violated. Meares and Kahan have discovered nothing new when they tell us, with the breathless enthusiasm of discovery, that the majority of law-abiding blacks—like the majority of law-abiding whites—want the police to have more power, the courts to stop freeing the guilty, and civil libertarians to mind their own suburban business.

Nor is there anything new about groups with agendas seeking to undercut inconvenient rights that interfere with those agendas. Recall the impatience many feminists had with the First Amendment's protection of pornography, or Jews with the First Amendment's protection of Nazi marchers and Holocaust deniers. Rights, especially for those suspected of doing or saying bad things, are always inconvenient and rarely garner the support of a majority of any community.

Taken to its logical conclusion, the Meares/Kahan hypothesis would allow a majority of believers in a given community to require Christian prayer in the public schools. After all, "because these dissenting [non-

Christian] individuals had every chance to voice their opposition in the political process, and because there is every reason to believe that the majority—whose members were affected in exactly the same way—give due weight to the dissenters' interests, there is no good reason for the courts to second-guess the community's determination that [compelled prayer] strike[s] a fair balance." The same could be said for a community that did not want *Playboy* magazine to be sold in neighborhood stores, or Communists or Jehovah's Witnesses to disturb its tranquillity.

Meares and Kahan prefer "group rights"—in this case the rights of a majority of law-abiding, black, inner-city residents—over individual rights—in this case the rights of individuals who do not wish to be subjected to random searches or be told when to go home. But "group rights" is an oxymoron. Groups, especially those with increasing political power, have interests and agendas, but they may not implement those interests and agendas by ignoring the rights of individuals, especially the rights of those within the group who are disempowered and despised.

Throughout their essay, Meares and Kahan use terms such as "the residents," "the individuals most intimately affected," "the community," "minority residents," and "these very citizens" to make the point that those who are most affected by the challenged police practices do, in fact, consent to them. But that is simply not true: if those who are searched give their consent, the search is *ipso facto* lawful. If those who are asked to go home after II P.M. willingly do so, there is no constitutional violation. The conflict occurs precisely because some individuals refuse to consent. It is their rights that come into conflict with majority interests. It is no answer to say they consented, unless we accept the proposition—rejected by all rights theories—that a majority can consent for an unwilling minority.

The Meares-Kahan approach is part of a dangerous new vocabulary of rights disguised to undercut the traditional approach taken by our Constitution not in the 1960s, but in the 1790s. Our traditional conception of rights is directed against *governmental* abuses. Rights are designed to limit the power of the state, especially the police. They are negative rights, limiting the powers of political authorities: "the *state* may *not* . . ." This conception of rights grows out of a fundamental lesson of history: that in the long run, abuses by the state are far more dangerous to liberty and democracy than individual criminal conduct, dangerous and disturbing as that conduct may be. Now there are those who would introduce a new vocabulary of positive-sounding rights: the right to be free from pornography and other forms of offensive speech; the right to life; the right to pray in schools; the right to be safe from criminals—even the right of a victim's family to see his or her murderer executed. The effect of these new positive-sounding rights is to trump traditional negative rights. The implications of this process are limitless. Creative lawyers can come up with an anti-right disguised as a positive right to counteract virtually every traditional right. That is why the Meares-Kahan approach is so dangerous, not only to the Fourth Amendment, but to the rest of the Bill of Rights as well.

Meares and Kahan ignore these legitimate concerns, preferring instead to erect the straw man of paternalism. I have never heard a genuine civil libertarian make the absurd and demeaning paternalistic argument attributed to us by Meares and Kahan:

> Civil libertarians have an answer to these questions, too: no. The judgment and "self-respect" of inner-city residents, they sometimes maintain, has been deformed by social deprivation. Consequently, they lack the capacity to make critical assessments of curfews, gang-loitering ordinances, building searches, and other similar policies.

The argument *I* make is that civil liberties must not be changed in every decade to serve the immediate interests (legitimate as they may be) of a majority of one particular community. I am prepared to accept the conclusion (unsupported as it may be) that the statutes and regulations supported by Meares and Kahan are good for a majority of inner-city blacks today. That is surely a factor in assessing their constitutionality. But there are other factors as well, including the long-term precedental impact of legitimizing such practices and undercutting centuries of development of rights and remedies. I am not siding with white "suburban residents." Indeed, my personal aesthetic favors curfews in my neighborhood, so long as they are not selectively enforced against minorities. But I want these laws judged not by a transient majority of one particular ethnic group, but in light of our long history of abuse of police discretion and the continuing danger of unchecked government power.

If Meares and Kahan are correct that rights established (or remedies strengthened) in the 1960s continue to have an impact (a negative one, in their view) in the 1990s, then it would seem to follow that rights abolished (or remedies curtailed) in the 1990s will continue to have an impact in the next century. Our framers wrote a Bill of Rights not for one decade or one group of citizens, but as an enduring limitation on government. Rights *are* intended to evolve with changing realities, and Meares and Kahan make a compelling case for rethinking the application of rights to certain specific ordinances, policies, and police actions. But in the process of such rethinking, we must reject their broadside attack on individual rights and their voguish notion that long-entrenched safeguards against excesses of state power should be subordinated to the transient interests of majorities (even majorities within minorities), over the valid objections of minorities (even minorities within minorities).

So let me end with a direct answer to the "real question" Meares and Kahan have put to civil libertarians:

"Why can't we trust residents of the inner-city to decide for themselves?" We can and should, just as we should for all other residents, provided that their decisions recognize the individual constitutional rights of those affected residents who disagree with the majority. That is what distinguishes rights from interests.

Getting It Right

JEAN BETHKE ELSHTAIN

*I*n the lingo of the 1960s: Right on! Meares and Kahan help to expose the tendentious bad faith that now all too often animates absolutist libertarians, who seem more interested in maintaining ideological purity than in dealing with concrete troubles. In a world of abstract and nigh-absolute rights, one need not make a concrete connection to a community—any community—and its needs, values, desires, and norms. There's more than a bit of condescension and paternalism in such a perspective, and Meares and Kahan help us to nail it down.

Their article is written clearly, but let's just survey the main points. Residents of "Chicago's low-income housing projects"—already, then, victims of liberal social engineering that was distorted horribly from its inception—now have the "right to be free from mass building searches." But there is only one problem: "an overwhelming majority of the residents *opposed* the ACLU's effort to block the building searches." This mattered not to the ACLU, which was determined to force "self-respect" upon people it clearly regards as less than competent citizens. Lurking in the interstices of this extraordinary idea is an utterly banal bit of what should have been discarded long ago: the Marxist canard about false consciousness. If "the people" make the wrong decisions, the theory went, it's because they cannot see what is right or in their own best interests—and therefore their judgment should be overridden. Meares and Kahan call this position "paradoxical." It is worse than that. It is unconscionable.

From here, one could take the argument in several directions. Perhaps the fruit was poisoned from the tree—that is, the ACLU from its very inception has dedicated itself to such an abstracted, view-from-nowhere notion of rights that this is par for the course. Or, alternatively, the ACLU may have become locked into more rigid categories over time, and now cannot see the forest for the trees. I would probably argue the second alternative in a longer treatment of this issue. Either way, though, the critical point is the same. Something has gone off the rails, and that something isn't the ordinary citizens who must live in circumstances and neighborhoods where the average ACLU litigator wouldn't want to spend an hour. It is, as Meares and Kahan say, the "prevailing understanding of rights" as "fashioned in the 1960s."

This prevalent view is that inner-city African-Americans need to be protected from government, especially the police. I admit that I held this view myself for a while. A wake-up call for me was hearing philosopher Cornel West insist that the overtaking of the inner-city black community by drugs and gangs pointed to malign neglect by civic authorities, including the failure to provide that community the protection *from violence* afforded routinely to white citizens. African-Americans are beset not only by episodes of "police brutality" but also by the widespread defection of civic authorities from hands-on concern for and protection of their security and well-being. Meares and Kahan point out that this "toleration of crime and disorder"—a not-so-benign neglect—"helped to accelerate urban decay" and to bring about the situation we know all too well today.

At the heart of this supposedly liberal attitude lay a deep suspicion of community or plural communities. That suspicion persists. Whenever I give a talk invoking the importance of strong, sturdy, viable communities and institutions, I inevitably get a question suggesting that I want the Ku Klux Klan (or the Montana Militia, or whatever) to run amok, or at least that somehow my position provides no remedy for that possibility. The logic behind such questions is a kind of Gresham's Law of politics and social life: bad community drives out good. It presumes that I would agree that organizations like the Klan or the Militia are serving to help constitute the basis of sturdy democratic community—which is absurd. It presumes that I want to repeal the Bill of

Rights and federal law enforcement, which is equally absurd. The more interesting questions are, Why the suspicion of communities and the self-constitution of citizens? Why the lurking fear that somehow citizens cannot, or will not, "get it right"? This is where the ACLU displays liberal condescension so consistently and troublingly.

Locked into a position that has become a frozen ideology—unable, it seems, to rethink its assumptions as any lively, decent, and (I would argue) *liberal* effort can and must—the ACLU becomes the tormentor of those it claims to serve. In her day, Hannah Arendt skewered the brokers of ideology, accusing them of what she found to be the worst of sins: thoughtlessness. People go on automatic pilot. They feel repeatedly confirmed in their own "idea." And they do careless and horrible things as a result. Why? Because they cannot take on an interlocutor. They begin from a few interlocked premises and then everything flows in a kind of terrible "logical" tyranny.

This, it seems, is how the ACLU reacts in many, if not the vast majority, of cases. The upshot? Residents of crime-ridden low-income housing in Chicago can be splendidly alone with their rights as they huddle indoors for safety. This is terrible because in civil society we relate not as "autonomous" entities but as members of communities and neighborhoods and crafts and jobs and enterprises. To deny people the necessary preconditions, including fundamental physical safety, to enable them to enact and to display projects that flow from their basic sociality is to deny them their full humanity. The ACLU long ago ceased to think politically and ethically about these matters; indeed, if Meares and Kahan are right—and I think they are—it has ceased to think, period.

It's Not So Simple

JOEL F. HANDLER

Let me begin with two stories from a bygone era.

The first comes from the 1960s. Back when we used to build public housing, a group of progressive architects asked prospective residents what kind of apartments they would like. Much to the puzzlement of the architects, most residents described a "railroad" flat, a string of rooms one behind the other with a front room where their daughters could entertain suitors. Then the architects had an idea. They built models of other kinds of apartments. This time the residents preferred the models. What happened, of course, is that when first asked, the residents reflected on how they grew up and did not have a vision of other possibilities.

The second story involves a study of unannounced caseworker visits to the homes of welfare recipients. Half the families in the study's sample had telephones, and the workers would call first to make an appointment; half did not have telephones, so the workers came unannounced. (This was an era of benign administration.) The group without the phones said that they did not mind the unannounced visits; on the other hand, the

group with the phones said that they would mind an unannounced visit very much. Again, the different answers
reflected different experiences.

The moral of these stories—which scholars and activists working with dependent people have known for a
long time—is that it is not always easy to ascertain what
people really want. One has to listen very carefully, and
recognize that power also operates indirectly—through
unspoken agendas and the subtle manipulations of so-
cialization. Which brings me to the essay by Meares and
Kahan. They are rightly concerned about paternalism,
but paternalism takes many forms. One might consider
where the people in question are coming from, and why.

Let's make the point less abstract. Meares and Kahan
present an appealing case. At least as they characterize
the facts, Chicago Housing Authority (CHA) residents
actively participated in a vigorous debate about the policing policies at issue. But what happens a year later?
Crime has gone down somewhat, some residents feel
more secure, others do not want to change the rules governing building searches or "sweeps." We know from
housing associations and school committees that atten-
dance at community meetings tends to decline over time
until a relatively few activists run the show. How would
Meares and Kahan (and the courts) decide whether it is
appropriate to allow "community burden-sharing" when
most of the affected people are not present, debating and
voting? The standard view is that if people do not attend,

it means they are not interested. But, as Jane Mansbridge pointed out in *Beyond Adversary Democracy*, there could be many reasons for non-attendance—some may feel that participation is futile, while others may think that their own interests are being adequately represented. Again, the point is that the test proposed by Meares and Kahan involves subtle and complex factual determinations that are not simple, one-time decisions.

Consider their argument that we do not have to worry as much as we used to about inappropriate use of discretionary powers by the authorities because African-Americans have elected positions in local government and now make up some proportion of police forces. For someone who (like me) lives in Los Angeles, this claim is truly amazing. Rodney King? Driving While Black? And it is not just this one city. Complaints about law enforcement discrimination against blacks continue to be heard loud and clear throughout the country.

The Meares/Kahan view of political accountability is also naive on another front. Blacks and Hispanics do not speak with one voice. And what about other minority groups? When I was growing up in the East, and working in the Midwest, I saw the world in terms of black and white: Los Angeles was an eye-opener. It reminded me that in our country we have a long history of racial hatred across and between many groups. Sadly, intra-group conflict was a major factor in the Los Angeles riots; most of the violence occurred in transitional neighborhoods.

But large public housing projects and other crime-vulnerable neighborhoods are often composed of many ethnic groups—a mixture of long-term residents and newly arrived immigrants. One can easily imagine minorities within larger minority groups feeling isolated and threatened—which, in turn, would substantially complicate our judgments about the accuracy and fairness of "community-based" decisions regarding sweeps and curfews.

Community empowerment is a laudable goal, and we should work towards it. But it is a subtle and complex process. It's not as simple as calling a town meeting.

More Wrong Than Rights

CAROL S. STEIKER

*W*hen I was a first-year law student, my contracts professor gave us the following hypothetical: You are drowning in a lake. A fellow walking along the shore calls out to you, "Hey, I've got a rope for sale." You shout desperately, "How much?" He replies, "A million dollars." If you accept and he throws you the rope, is that a valid contract?

The professor wanted to discuss the necessary "background conditions" for valid consent. We learned that contract law sometimes recognizes the inequities of the real (in addition to the hypothetical) world, and sometimes refuses to hold people to the "unconscionable" agreements into which they may have entered.[1] This aspect of contract law acknowledges something we all know from experience: life is full of hard choices, and some are so hard that it does not seem accurate to call them "choices" at all. Remember the old Jack Benny routine. Benny, famous for and famously humorous about his cheapness, is held up at gunpoint by a mugger who says, "Your money or your life!" After a long silence, the mugger says, "Well?" And Benny replies, "I'm thinking, I'm thinking."

What is true about the law of commercial contracts is true as well about the social contract writ large, and this truth illuminates the major problem underlying the argument of Dan Kahan and Tracey Meares about policing in the inner city. Meares and Kahan urge that the "consent"—through elected representatives—of a substantial proportion of the residents of poor minority neighborhoods should validate such police practices as "suspicionless" searches of their homes, nighttime curfews for their children, and anti-loitering ordinances that permit the police to order the dispersal of certain groups congregating in public places. Surely these communities are smart enough to know what will help them the most, argue Meares and Kahan; outside agitators like the ACLU should stand aside and stop trying to foist "unwanted rights" on neighborhoods ravaged by drugs, gangs, and violence.

The fallacy here is that, even by the rosy account offered by Meares and Kahan, the purported consent of the communities in question looks suspiciously like that of the desperate swimmer grabbing the rope. Meares and Kahan acknowledge that minority communities have long been the victims of discriminatory law enforcement. They note that the police historically have underprotected inner-city communities from crime, while simultaneously subjecting inner-city residents—primarily young African-American and Hispanic males—to especially intrusive and violent tactics. Meares and Kahan frankly recognize that "society at large refuses to address the social inequities at the root of inner-city crime," and they hold out little hope for change on that score: "Thirty years' worth of real-world experience belies the idea that spiraling inner-city crime will somehow force powerful interests *outside* the inner city to revitalize these communities." Under these circumstances, it is ridiculous to suggest that inner-city residents would affirmatively choose to trade away their civil liberties; but other investments in neighborhood security—like better conventional policing, more economic opportunity, improved schools, or safer housing—are simply not available. In dire straits, and with limited options, they will grasp at any rope, no matter how steep the price. What is more, the history that Meares and Kahan recite demonstrates not only that inner-city residents are desperately struggling in a sea of crime, but also that we—"society at large"—through years of discriminatory neglect and abuse, have pushed them in. We are not only taking unconscionable advantage of their circumstances; we bear some of the responsibility for those circumstances.

Not to worry, console Meares and Kahan. Law enforcement might once have been neglectful and even abusive of minority communities in the inner city, but that history is—well, history. Meares and Kahan point to the impressive gains that African-Americans have made in political representation on both national and local levels. In light of this progress, they argue, we should view support by minority communities for voluntarily curtailing their own civil rights and empowering the police as a sign of political empowerment rather than desperation. If minority communities do not fear overreaching or bias by the police (or if they fear these things less than they fear crime), who are we—or the ACLU— to gainsay them? In a nutshell (they claim), the background conditions of inequality that would make us doubt the freedom of minority communities to "consent" to onerous law enforcement tactics have been eradicated. The swimmer is not drowning; rather, she is doing the backstroke.

This rosy picture is utterly implausible. Yes, African-Americans have made some impressive gains in political representation. (Note that Meares and Kahan make no mention of Hispanics on this score.) But these gains have not, as Meares and Kahan acknowledge, led to any greater willingness on the part of "society at large" to pump resources into the inner cities. Nor has discriminatory law enforcement been anywhere close to eradicated. There is a burgeoning literature documenting the disparate enforcement of traffic laws against minority motorists, creating a phenomenon now widely and derisively known as "DWB"—Driving While Black. And recent high-profile cases of police abuses, like those of

Malice Green in Detroit and Abner Louima in New York, sadly document how far we still must go to get to the world that Meares and Kahan imagine we live in today—one in which the relationship between the police and minorities is no longer presumptively antagonistic. Indeed, the fact that huge numbers of African-American men are in prison or under the supervision of the criminal justice system—which Meares and Kahan use to illustrate the rationality of trading civil rights for more policing—demonstrates just how ineffectual the increased political power of African-Americans has been in improving the circumstances of the most impoverished minority communities.

But let us assume for a moment, however implausibly, that Meares and Kahan are right about the background conditions. Let us imagine that African-Americans have achieved so much political power, and that racially discriminatory law enforcement has become so much a thing of the past, that their "consent" to onerous law enforcement initiatives could be respected as voluntary. Would that be the end of the argument? No, and for two further powerful reasons.

First, not only are Meares and Kahan wrong about the background conditions and thus about the validity of the consent at issue, they are also wrong about the very *existence* of the consent. For example, Meares and Kahan strongly support the city of Chicago's gang-loitering ordinance, which gives Chicago police the authority to order the dispersal of any group "loitering" in public "with no apparent purpose" if a police officer reasonably suspects that one person in the group is a gang member. In their defense of the ordinance, Meares and Kahan observe that it was "passed by an overwhelming margin in the Chicago City Council, with key support from aldermen representing the city's most impoverished, crime-ridden districts, whose residents are predominantly members of racial and ethnic minorities." What this careful language conceals is that while the ordinance enjoyed the support of the overwhelming majority of the city's white aldermen, it got the support of only six of the city's eighteen *black* aldermen.[2] And while Meares and Kahan filed an amicus brief arguing for the constitutionality of the ordinance on behalf of some inner-city neighborhood organizations, an amicus brief was also filed on the other side by such individuals and organizations as U.S. Representative Jesse Jackson, Jr., the NAACP, the National Council of La Raza, and the Chicago Alliance for Neighborhood Safety.

The story of the Chicago gang-loitering ordinance is typical. The majority community, "society at large," tends to overwhelmingly support loosening the restraints that the Constitution has been held to place on the police because they know that the burdens of such enhanced "discretion" in policing will fall disproportionately on minority citizens. Minority communities tend to be far more divided. Gallup poll after Gallup poll shows that African-Americans trust the police less and fear them more than white people do, and this ambivalence is reflected in decisions on matters of policy. Very often, as in the case of the Chicago ordinance, nothing like a majority of minority citizens supports the policy at issue. And even when a majority does, there is always substantial dissent (as in the 30 percent of African-American teens who did not endorse curfews for juveniles in the Washington, D.C., poll mentioned by Meares and Kahan). Minority communities, like all other communities in "society at large," are not unitary and do not speak in one voice. Rights are personal and can be waived, as Meares and Kahan are quick to point out. But why should a minority—or even a majority of a minority—be permitted to waive the rights of *everyone* in the community?

Which brings me to my final objection. Suppose Meares and Kahan are right about both issues discussed above: suppose a real majority of the residents of inner-city neighborhoods supported some onerous policing initiative and suppose background conditions were such that we should respect and enforce that consent. There are still good reasons to invalidate the kinds of policing initiatives the authors support. Our laws do not permit people to sell their children, their bodily organs, or themselves into slavery. These prohibitions reflect, at least in part, the idea that some things are too important to be alienated. Freedom from certain kinds of law enforcement tactics should be on anyone's short list. Police searches of homes without good reason to suspect individual inhabitants of wrongdoing and police regulation of public spaces through curfews and orders of dispersal have always been disfavored under the Fourth Amendment[3]—not only because such policies can be tools of racial oppression, but also because the privacy of the home and the freedom to travel and congregate in public spaces are thought, rightly, to be essential to a free people in a democracy. Justice Jackson said it best:

Fourth Amendment freedoms . . . are not mere second-class rights but belong in the catalog of indispensable freedoms. Among deprivations of rights, none is so effective in cowing a population, crushing the spirit of the individual and putting terror in every heart. Uncontrolled search and seizure is one of the first and most effective weapons in the arsenal of every arbitrary government. And one need only briefly to have dwelt and worked among a people possessed of many admirable qualities but deprived of these rights to know that the human personality deteriorates and dignity and self-reliance disappear where homes, persons and possessions are subject at any hour to unheralded search and seizure by the police.[4]

These "indispensable freedoms"—like all rights that trump expedient policy—have a price tag. Policing is more difficult and more costly without suspicionless searches and seizures, curfews, loitering laws, and the like. But if we permitted the felt exigencies of the time as expressed by strong majoritarian sentiment to prevail, the special status of Fourth Amendment freedoms as *constitutional* freedoms would be jeopardized. Here Justice Marshall said it best: "History teaches us that grave threats to liberty often come in times of urgency, when constitutional rights seem too extravagant to endure."[5]

Urgent though the times undoubtedly are, and "wrong" as Fourth Amendment rights might seem to some in their inhibiting power, some things are more wrong than these rights.

Everybody's Business

WESLEY G. SKOGAN

*I*t's a brave act for Meares and Kahan to step forward at this moment with these arguments. As this contribution to the New Democracy Forum series was being finalized, major newspapers were giving daily front-page coverage to the case of an immigrant to New York City named Amadou Diallo, killed by a hail of bullets because he acted furtively when confronted in his foyer by a band of armed men in plain clothes. The story quickly became a focus for debate about the legitimacy of New York's apparently effective crime prevention program, one based on aggressive order maintenance tactics that push the envelope when it comes to lawful police intrusion into the lives of loitering, sauntering, hustling, and "signifying" young men on the street. As protesters tried in vain to penetrate the riot barriers surrounding City Hall, Meares and Kahan were assuring us that proactive order maintenance is fine—as long as the community is ready to bear with it and police are capable of being smart about it.

They think it can work because African-Americans (the only group they really consider) have enough power

in enough places to ensure that police will really work on
their behalf; that communities can deliberate and decide
when their crime problems are so overwhelming that
they need to call friendly fire down upon themselves; that
society's only other response will be even more repres-
sion; and that police on the street will be able to "fine-
tune" their practices well enough so that only the bad
guys will be seriously discomforted.

Maybe. To their credit, Meares and Kahan do not
duck consideration of the most problematic practices,
those involving stops, searches, and arrests. These lie
close to the core of the police function, which involves
the legitimate use of violence. But I think their argument
would be stronger if they linked their appeal to another
policing strategy that is also on the minds of many: community policing. Community policing has vast political
appeal, so much that scarcely a police chief, mayor, or
city manager in the country wants to be caught without it. A thoroughgoing community policing program
also provides structures and processes that could form a
solid underpinning for both general principles of what
Meares and Kahan call 1990s-style rights: that a community can deliberate and decide what policies are right
for its members, and that discretionary order maintenance by police can be responsive to the concerns of the
law-abiding people of a neighborhood.

One feature of a serious community policing program
is that neighborhood residents are involved in identi-

fying and prioritizing local crime problems, through a constructive dialogue with one another and with police officers who work in their immediate area. In Chicago this takes place at public meetings held monthly in each of the city's 279 local police beats. At these meetings, both police and citizens also report on what they have accomplished since the last meeting and what they will work on next. Residents criticize police actions, and since the officers who attend work in the neighborhood every day and will be back at the next month's meeting, they cannot miss or ignore the message. These meetings often include debates over how police should respond to order maintenance problems, and Meares and Kahan have it right that inner-city residents need and desperately want help from the police in reclaiming their communities. Because departments that practice community policing have been reorganized around small, neighborhood beats, their officers develop a great deal of community-specific knowledge that they are able to apply to their problem solving. Community policing involves decentralizing responsibility as well as authority to these local teams, and their sergeants become the most important people in the department—they represent the level where the buck has to stop if a fine-tuned exercise of discretion is to be the order of the day.

In short, community policing can provide an organizational framework for dialogue and decision making, a forum for securing month-in, month-out accountability to residents for what beat officers are doing to apply local solutions to local problems, and a management structure that gives it a chance to actually work.

Would any of this have helped Amadou Diallo? He was shot by a roving tactical team that would never have recognized him as a local street peddler, and finding ways to involve detectives, the drug squad, and SWAT teams in community policing has been a struggle for departments nationwide. The SWAT team in particular is where the aggressive young hotshots want to go, and where a lot of problems with the community arise. In Chicago, officers committed to beat work have complained that these "cowboys" fail to keep faith with the neighborhoods where the beat cops work every day. Washington, D.C., has probably made the most dramatic move toward reining in the SWAT teams, by forcing virtually every unit in the department to decentralize into the city's service areas and get involved in dialogue with community residents. The jury is still out on whether Washington can make it stick, but this move reveals that police managers know that community policing has to be the entire department's program and not just something handed off to "wave and smile" units.

A fair objection to community policing is that the constructive dialogue component of this kind of program takes place outside the political system. Fewer people get involved than turn out to vote, and nobody elected the decision makers. But neighborhood safety is not about taxing and spending, it is about ensuring the quality of a service. Neighborhood issues and concerns are too local for a formal political system, and this is one reason for the popularity of community policing. Although as a recent immigrant, Amadou Diallo was not eligible to vote, he could have spoken up at beat meetings: as they say in Chicago, "Safe streets are everybody's business."

Twice Victimized

MARGARET A. BURNHAM

*T*racey Meares and Dan Kahan have simply got it wrong. To use poor black Chicagoans as guinea pigs for enhanced police powers of dubious constitutionality is to twice victimize their communities.

Although Meares and Kahan purport to be speaking up for crime-besieged project dwellers, whose plight they say is made worse by patronizing, non-ghetto-dwelling civil libertarians, the proposals they endorse have for decades been advanced in the Supreme Court, among other venues. In fact, the post-Warren Court has steadily eroded the probable cause requirement of the Fourth Amendment by permitting officers to conduct limited street searches on suspicion and unfettered car searches without a warrant. The Fourth Amendment jurisprudence of the 1960s that the authors claim is outmoded no longer really exists. It has been eviscerated by a Court that has been swayed by twenty years of conservative politics aimed at racially polarizing the electorate around the issue of crime. When coupled with today's vastly more intrusive search tools, the trend in the Burger and Rehnquist Courts to accede to law enforcement claims of necessity has meant that the police now enjoy enormous powers to stop and frisk citizens on the street, or to search their cars, homes, and offices. Chicago's 1992 anti-gang ordinance, and its housing authority's mass building search policy are hardly new, innovative law enforcement strategies; rather they are just a further slide along the same slope.

The fact that some black constituencies and their elected representatives have sponsored these proposals should not make them more acceptable. In 1982, Justice Thurgood Marshall, chiding his colleagues for their willingness to make exceptions to Fourth Amendment constraints in car cases, wrote in *United States v. Ross* that "[t]he Court derives satisfaction from the fact that its rule does not exalt the rights of the wealthy over the rights of the poor. A rule so broad that all citizens lose vital Fourth Amendment protection is no cause for celebration." As Marshall's words suggest, although rights define the individual's relation to the state, each person's rights are no greater than those possessed by every other individual. A lowered constitutional bar affects not only those rejecting protections against arbitrary or discriminatory practices for themselves, but everyone else as well. Thus the Chicago housing project rule will quickly apply wherever the police want to conduct indiscriminate searches. The Chicago ordinance criminalizing the act of "remain[ing] in any one place with no apparent purpose" while in the company of a gang member may be used to throttle political dissent, or to rid city streets of "undesirables."

The idea that insular poor black communities should be allowed to opt out of constitutional rules—even those developed to protect racial minorities—has also come up in the context of public education. Many cities, including Chicago, have sought to establish all-black, all-male schools in order to better address the unique challenges these youths must contend with. Proponents argue that as long as integrated co-ed schools are also available, these separate institutions should be deemed lawful because their mission is to challenge rather than perpetuate social disadvantages. It is questionable whether the exclusion of black girls is necessary to accomplish this mission, but in any event, the argument that available alternatives render constitutional infringements less pernicious can hardly be applied to the Chicago criminal justice measures. Families who don't consent to the blanket searches can't just pick up stakes and move to the suburbs, and youths with legitimate reasons, even frivolous ones, to go out at night can't do so with a curfew in place.

I have two further problems with the Meares and Kahan thesis. The first is their tendency to understate the harm such proposals would likely do to these communities. They ignore the continuing reality of racially motivated police abuse, and they suggest that black inclusion in police work has radically altered the hostile relationship this community has historically had with the police. But it is dangerous to expand police search and arrest powers in the very communities most victimized by police use of race as a proxy for criminality. Because discrimination tends to be institutional, subtle, and unconscious, even the black Officer Friendly relies on deeply ingrained stereotypes of what a criminal looks like. Racially motivated police misconduct does not appear to be on the wane, as Meares and Kahan seem to suggest, but rather it is an inevitable consequence of the new "zero tolerance" policies of big-city departments, exemplified most dramatically by the Amadou Diallo shooting in New York City. These clean-sweep policies could not have been adopted if the Supreme Court had not relaxed Fourth Amendment search requirements. As far back as 1968, the ever-prescient Justice William Brennan wrote a note of caution to Chief Justice Earl Warren about the dangers of permitting the police to stop and frisk on less than probable cause:

I've become acutely concerned that . . . our affirmance in *Terry* [the stop and frisk case] will be taken by police . . . as our license to them to . . . widely expand, present "aggressive surveillance," techniques which the press tells us are being deliberately employed in . . . ghetto cities. This is happening, of course, in response to the "crime in the streets" alarums being sounded in this election year. . . . [There is a] terrible risk that police will conjure up "suspicious circumstances," and courts will credit their versions.[1]

Thirty years after Brennan articulated the basis for what Meares and Kahan term "community distrust" and "discretion skepticism," we are all waiting with baited breath to hear what "suspicious circumstances" led New York officers to shoot Diallo forty-one times. DWB—"driving while black"—is not a 1960s expression but a 1990s one.

Some would contend that a tragedy like the Diallo homicide is the price that must be paid for improved public safety in New York, and Meares and Kahan suggest that project dwellers should be allowed to strike that balance in their own communities. But making law on the basis of a cost-benefit analysis applied to search and arrest practices would destroy the core constitutional guarantee of equal and individualized treatment with regard to the use of police power. The "burden-sharing test" the authors propose merely shifts to beleaguered communities the burden of restraint that the Constitution imposes upon the state. Moreover, as we have seen, the real price of New York's "zero tolerance" policies is not just one horrific police homicide but a pervasive sense of insecurity and powerlessness in the black community.

The second false premise of the authors' thesis is that there are no reasonably effective law enforcement alternatives to proposals that diminish constitutional protections. They wrongly suggest that drastic solutions are necessary because failures in policing have contributed to an alarming increase in crime in minority communities. The fact is that serious crime by blacks is not increasing but rather has remained level for more than ten years. What has increased since criminal justice policy became a political marker is the disproportion in punishment along racial lines. The number of black prisoners since 1980 has tripled. Recent studies demonstrate that this disproportion in sentencing is the foreseeable and invidious consequence of the politics of the 1980s and the resultant so-called War on Drugs.

The authors put forth the Chicago proposals as an alternative to the inhumane Reagan-Bush policies that have resulted in the stark increase in rates of incarceration, particularly for minorities. But it is naive to think that these proposals will supplant more draconian measures. More likely, by criminalizing whole communities —innocent young men for curfew violations, apartment dwellers for petty offenses like marijuana possession— the Chicago proposals will transform benign behavior into criminal conduct. Rather than using arbitrary procedures that disproportionately burden minorities, policy analysts should continue to focus on reducing sentencing and other disparities. Moreover, we would do well to follow the lead of other Western nations, such as Great Britain and Germany, and build treatment centers instead of more jails.

The authors might roll their eyes in disdain at such an outdated concept. Their approach to the crisis in criminal justice bears a striking resemblance to that of critics of affirmative action, some black, who decry race-conscious remedies as no longer necessary and as harmful to the intended beneficiaries. Beneath the surface of their appeal is the contested territory of the role of race in current public policy—beliefs about the proper meaning of civil rights, the proper weight to be given to historical discrimination, the proper policy tools for dealing with individual choice and race bias. But as the affirmative action debate teaches, short-sighted solutions to intractable problems are not valid just because some black voices support them. The measures that Meares and Kahan advocate are not so much about expanding black self-determination as they are about extending an already discredited approach to crime.

A Multi-Problem Theory

FRANKLIN E. ZIMRING

I have no doubt that Tracey Meares and Dan Kahan are sincere in their enthusiasm for curfews, anti-gang loitering ordinances, and other currently popular methods of exercising social control over the young in urban areas. Yet I am reminded of Oscar Wilde's insight about sincerity—a great deal of it can be positively fatal.

Let me organize my substantial reservations about the Meares/Kahan analysis around four issues: 1) the "crime context" for constitutional theory, 2) the problematic characterization of 1960s-style constitutional rights, 3) the unpersuasive then-and-now analysis of the relationship between African-Americans and urban street police, and 4) the mysterious principles the authors put forth as 1990s-style constitutional safeguards.

1. Fear of Crime as Basis for Constitutional Theory. As part of their critique of a rights-based theory of criminal procedure, Meares and Kahan tell us that

[c]rime in minority communities has also changed dramatically since the 1960s: it has grown substantially worse. While national crime rates have been steadily declining during the past decade, they have been *increasing* in the predominantly minority neighborhoods of America's inner cities [italics in original].

I regard this passage as wrong on two counts. In the first place, the rate of serious crime in the inner cities has *not* been increasing over the past decade. Big-city crime rates in general have declined over that period, and although for most categories of crime city-level rates are not available by race, the most important, and reliable, indicator is homicide, about which race-specific statistics do exist. Between 1986 and 1996, the homicide rate for African-Americans declined by 20 percent, according to FBI figures.[1] I have no idea how or why the authors believe otherwise. The increase in the numbers of African-Americans in prison and on probation that they cite is a product of more punitive policies and huge increases in drug punishments. It is not due to an increase in the crime rate.

The second error is turning crime trends into constitutional arguments. Meares and Kahan show why crime is a bad thing for communities, but they don't tell us explicitly much about why the rate of crime at a particular moment should enter into the constitutional calculus. Is this just an indirect version of the usual argument that civil liberties hamper the government in its pursuit of wrongdoers? If so, I would remind the authors that this appeal has a long and unpleasant history, in the United States and elsewhere. Further, since any amount of murder and rape is too much, there is no reason to suppose that popular sympathies would shift in favor of reducing police powers should crime levels drop. Right-wingers typically turn civil liberties issues into referenda on whether citizens are afraid of violent crime. There is nothing peculiar to the 1990s in this ploy, nor are there any limits to the types of expanded police powers it can be enlisted to support.

2. *Getting the 1960s Wrong.* The portrait of the Warren Court's approach to the balance between civil liberties and public order painted by Meares and Kahan is grossly misleading. Their article tells us that this Court displayed "discretion skepticism," but the only case from the Warren Court's body of work they cite to this specific effect is *Papachristou*, an opinion which struck down criminal loitering statutes.

And how would Meares and Kahan incorporate the opinion in *Terry v. Ohio* into their vision of the Warren Court as anti-discretionary? Decided by an eight-to-one majority in 1968, this case allowed police officers who lacked probable cause to frisk the subjects of street encounters for weapons if the officers had a reasonable suspicion that a weapon might be present. The majority opinion, which provided an open-ended doctrinal approach to problems of safety in the streets, was written by Earl Warren himself. It was a leading indicator of the balancing style that justifies weapons-screening in airports and other public places.

Why did the Court strike down a vague loitering statute in *Papachristou* but uphold discretionary weapons-frisking by police operating without explicit statutory authority? Perhaps because the justices felt that the threat of armed suspects was substantial and the limited frisking privilege was a response that did not go further than the risks demanded. The "void for vagueness" doctrine of *Papachristou* dealt with citizen behaviors that were much less threatening, and with legislative prohibitions that were unnecessarily broad and unclear.

Whatever the true relationship between these two decisions, the "Warren Court" described by Meares and Kahan could never have written *Terry v. Ohio*. And *Terry* is just the beginning. The most eloquent refutation of Meares and Kahan can be found by reading the entire body of cases on criminal procedure decided by the Court during Warren's tenure as chief justice.

3. Police Discretion through African-American Eyes. The authors play out their 1960s-versus-1990s contrast in an attempt to validate a Chicago statute that gives individual police officers the power to decide what groups might include a gang member and the legal authority to disperse any such group at pain of criminal liability. In this context, all the data about African-American political power and diversity in city policing in the Meares and Kahan article seem to argue that most African-American adults would be happy if urban police had this kind of power over African-American kids.

In the aftermath of the Rodney King and O. J. Simpson episodes, a new willingness of the part of significant groups of African-Americans in central cities to trust their local police is not a matter I am prepared to take on faith. From this perspective, the Meares and Kahan analysis is disappointing in three respects. First, they do not zero in on police discretion when discussing the changing elements of African-American participation in urban governance. Second, they present no evidence on the question of African-American attitudes toward discretionary police power. Third, there is no mention of either the O. J. Simpson or Rodney King episodes as indicators of African-American public opinion about police powers and conduct.

4. The Mystery Apparatus. The Meares and Kahan article puts forward two new principles as relevant to standards of constitutional review—"burden-sharing" and "guided discretion." My deferral of these issues is a function of my ignorance: I do not know what these two concepts denote, and I do not know how finding either or both of these elements present is supposed to alter constitutional decision making. Herewith a few of the mysteries.

On burden-sharing: What group must share the burden? Is it all African-Americans, African-American men, all younger men? What is the relevant community in a plural society? Who decides whether sufficient burden-sharing exists? What should be the consequence of this finding for the constitutional test? On guided discretion: What elements of the Chicago statute Meares and Kahan support constitutes *guided* discretion? Who are the guides? Who decides whether the guidance is sufficient, using what standards?

I would know more about the content of either key phrase if Meares and Kahan gave examples of current proposals that would flunk these tests. In their current analysis, however, burden-sharing and guided discretion sound more like after-the-fact support for the gang-loitering statute than an independently derived set of constitutional principles. For this reason, the article sounds more like a moot court exercise than a theory articulating when political majorities ought to be allowed to expand the powers that police can exercise on city streets.

Maybe their moot court argument is a winner. Perhaps the theme song for crime control in the late 1990s will be "Anything Goes." My hope, however, is that the (never particularly popular) Bill of Rights will continue to function in the ways that have improved the quality of American society for generations.

Inalienable Rights

JEREMY WALDRON

Since I suspect that the points I propose to make in response to the Meares and Kahan critique of rights may be in danger of being dismissed as "unduly abstract," "outmoded," merely "semantic," and evidence of legal "scholasticism," perhaps I should start by suggesting that we avoid that sort of dismissive rhetoric. After all, the authors acknowledge towards the end of their article that the issues they address are complex and delicate, and that no one thinks rights are altogether unimportant. If that is so, there might be virtue in not trying to discredit up front those who wish to be a little more thoughtful about the dangers of alienating our rights than they are.

I use the word "alienating" advisedly, because the issue is whether constitutional rights—such as the Fourth Amendment right to be secure against unreasonable searches and seizures—should be regarded as *inalienable* or not. "Inalienable" is not just a pretty word inserted by Thomas Jefferson into the Declaration of Independence for rhetorical effect. It means rights that may not be given away by those who have them, and therefore that no system of absolute power may ever be defended on the ground that reasonable people would have found it prudent, in certain circumstances, to alienate these rights. Meares and Kahan say that "we ordinarily think of rights as belonging to individuals," with the implication that therefore, of course, these rights can be sold or bargained away like any other form of property. In fact, there was a century or two of controversy in early modern rights theory about that very point. Some sixteenth-century theorists defended slavery, for example, on what we would recognize as Hobbesian grounds: it would be rational for a person or a whole people to sell themselves into subjection in order to better preserve their lives and security. Insistence on the inalienability of rights was a way of opposing such contracts, and it was this opposing conception—the idea of rights held in trust and the right-bearer as steward rather than owner of his rights—that triumphed in works of John Locke and the formulations of Thomas Jefferson. I am afraid this understanding is more than two hundred years older than the "1960s understanding" that Meares and Kahan dismiss as anachronistic, but it may be worth bearing in mind.

Alienating a right is different from choosing to exercise or waive it in a particular case. A police officer comes to my door and asks to look around my apartment; if I give my permission, I have waived my Fourth Amendment right. But the next time he comes, he must ask again, and if he is refused he cannot rely on my previous permission. He must seek a warrant, and the grounds for his search must be reasonable. Now one can view this as a difference in degree. But from the facts laid out in the Meares/Kahan article, it seems that what they are talking about is an alienation of the right to be free from unreasonable searches, not just a waiver in a particular instance. The Chicago Housing Authority's tenants— or "an overwhelming majority" of them—agreed in advance that their apartments are to be open indefinitely to mass searches whenever the police or the housing authority wish to conduct them. An analogy perhaps would be the difference between waiving one's right to trial by jury on a particular charge and agreeing in advance—say, upon graduation from high school—that one would not have the right to trial by jury for any charge or indictment in the future.

Meares and Kahan fail to notice that there is all the difference in the world between a voluntary waiver in a single instance and a general abandonment of one's rights. They couch the issue purely in terms of voluntariness. They quite rightly resist any suggestion that poor people are incapable of giving consent, or that poverty undermines voluntariness or corrodes the conditions of its meaningful exercise. These are certainly important issues so far as particular waivers of rights are concerned, but in the case of the wholesale alienation of rights, consent is not the issue. These are rights people hold as a legacy from the past and as a trust for the future. And that's not just rhetoric, either. Meares and Kahan trace a change in social circumstances over a couple of decades, by which rights that used to be important bulwarks against oppression have now ceased to be so. Do they imagine that there will not be changes in the future in the reverse direction? Do they think it unimaginable that public housing tenants will need to reclaim their right to be secure against unreasonable searches if the rather delicate safeguards that Meares and Kahan propose collapse or if racial attitudes change again for the worse? And are they asking us to believe that it will be as easy for the tenants or their successors to take these rights up again as it was to abandon them? I am not saying that the answers are obvious. But it is disturbing that Meares and Kahan do not even raise these questions, and that the only thing they have to say to the issue of inalienability is that it is unacceptably paternalistic to raise it—as if the indefinite waiver of a right by a whole class of persons had no effect on anyone but themselves.

I don't mean to suggest that rights should be immutable. In fact, I agree with the general drift of the Meares and Kahan analysis: we should be less panic-stricken than we sometimes are about democratic decisions in this area. But there is an important difference between a public, legislative, or constitutional debate about what rights are appropriate for the new millennium and the abandonment of certain rights by communities of tenants in housing projects. In a national debate, we can give some substance to the assurances that Meares and

Kahan offer about equal representation and about the chance for opposing voices to be heard. But there is something disconcerting about the alacrity with which these authors embrace the informal majoritarianism of community alienation. They say nothing about the number of the minority hold-outs. They say nothing about the effect of their opposition—are the minority now liable to the searches because of majority support for them? And they say nothing about the circumstances in which this support is elicited and obtained. Does one sign a form as a condition of getting a lease? Or is one's eligibility for public housing secure quite independently of whether one gives permission for mass searches? Again, I don't know the answers to these questions. But I am troubled by an article that does not even ask them, writing off any opposing voice as "a 'theological discourse' divorced from 'the life of the nation.'"

Matrioshka Dolls

BERNARD E. HARCOURT

*W*ho should decide whether a given police practice or local ordinance—like a housing authority policy permitting mass building searches, a youth curfew, or an anti-loitering measure—interferes with individual and social interests to such an extent that it is prohibited by the U.S. Constitution? Meares and Kahan offer a provocative answer: the specific community that is most directly and immediately burdened by the practice or ordinance in question. If that community supports the measure, Meares and Kahan write, then "the courts should presume . . . that the law does not violate individual rights." And as long as there is political accountability to that community, the courts need apply only a low level of scrutiny in evaluating the discretionary powers afforded the police. In effect, Meares and Kahan propose that the political process within the burdened community should determine the contours of constitutional rights with regard to criminal procedure.

Meares and Kahan talk about rights in a bold and refreshing way. For Meares and Kahan, rights are contextual—they depend on social and political conditions.

They are also instrumental. They can be deployed to empower certain groups. Rights are flexible, even unpre-
dictable—they change with different political climates.
Finally, rights are political. There is, ultimately, no
guarantee that a particular community will not dispense
with individual rights entirely. After all, mass building
searches cut a broad swath through traditional constitutional constraints governing criminal procedure.

As a result, their essay is likely to provoke passionate
resistance from liberals, whether rights foundationalists
or dual democrats—and especially from civil libertarians. After all, Meares and Kahan challenge a fundamental axiom of liberalism: the idea that constitutional
rights trump the ordinary democratic process—that
rights are inalienable, or foundational, or neutral, or (for
dual democrats) higher law. In this regard, I support
their endeavor. Their approach allows for more open debate about the values that underlie the finding of a right.
It may encourage judicial transparency and promote
greater opportunities for public criticism.

Nevertheless, their essay troubles me.

MORE NUANCE

To begin with, there are too many different voices within
African-American communities to attribute one posi-
tion to African-Americans, as Meares and Kahan do.
Inner-city communities themselves may be divided.

And this raises a host of thorny questions. How exactly do we define "the burdened community"? In the case of mass building searches in the Chicago housing projects, the answer is easy: residents of the CHA's projects. But what about youth curfews or anti-loitering ordinances? Meares and Kahan discuss the growth in African-American political strength and the rate of crime in African-American communities. Are African-Americans to be designated as the burdened community? If so, how do we define "the African-American community"? And how do we measure community sentiment? Should we rely on elected representatives of the community, on community leaders, or on a community-wide referendum? I doubt that we can even agree on an adequate definition of the community that is most directly and immediately burdened by youth curfews or anti-loitering ordinances. But regardless, it is incumbent on Meares and Kahan to address these difficult questions sooner rather than later—especially since theirs is a political-process theory.

Second, the views expressed within the inner city—as well as the views expressed in the more affluent suburbs—may well be influenced by crime, income, and race relations. Judge Wayne Anderson, according to Meares and Kahan, "dismissed the residents' willingness to consent to building searches as evidence of the corrosive effect of poverty and crime on their own 'self-respect.'" The authors in turn dismiss Judge Anderson for being paternalistic. But of course Judge Anderson is being paternalistic. He is being just as paternalistic as Meares and Kahan, who intimate, through the voice of Edna Pemberton, that residents who fear racial harassment have succumbed to "an ACLU scare tactic." These are paternalistic arguments. They are claims about false consciousness. But that does not mean we should ignore them.

Judge Anderson has put his finger on an extremely troubling issue. Cornel West discusses it in terms of "the profound sense of psychological depression, personal worthlessness, and social despair so widespread in black America."[1] We need to engage Judge Anderson and demand self-criticism from everyone involved—in the inner-city, in the affluent suburbs, at the courthouse, and among ourselves. We should ask ourselves how poverty and crime have shaped our own conceptions of ourselves and of our various communities.

Third, Meares and Kahan group together under one umbrella such varied measures and practices as mass building searches, youth curfews, anti-loitering ordinances, and "the like." Deciding whether or not any one specific measure or law enforcement practice is effective and worthwhile is extremely complex.[2] The authors concede that "reasonable people can disagree" about any given policy. But I would urge the authors not to lump these policies and methods together without sufficient attention to the differences between and among them.

MORE DEMOCRACY

Still, Meares and Kahan pose some powerful questions. The level of crime in the inner city deprives its residents of certain freedoms—their freedom to play in playgrounds, to feel secure in their schools, and to go out of their homes at night. As a result, they may feel that their civil rights are meaningless and they may be prepared to forego those rights if they believe that proposed law enforcement practices will reduce crime. Why should they not be allowed to make that informed decision? And why should residents of more affluent suburbs—whose freedoms are not curtailed in the same way—be allowed to block the inner-city residents from making that decision? Those questions have no easy answer.

But the solution is not to devolve the decision-making process to the inner-city residents. This proposal is not democratic enough. Policing techniques shape us all, and for that reason we all have a stake in the matter— not simply because the police might extend a practice outside the inner-city but because the very existence of practices that impinge upon basic rights affects all of us. We are all shaped by the policing practices that we, as a society, condone, witness, experience, and inflict. Mass building searches in the inner city are going to change our conceptions of privacy, authority, political power, and citizenship. Youth curfew laws are going to impact the cultural and intellectual lives of our children. Anti-loitering ordinances will have an effect on street life—of which there is scarcely any left in many cities. They will result in police records for more citizens and contribute to legal, or extra-legal, disenfranchisement.

For some, this is all for the better. The only issue before us, though, is whether inner-city residents alone should be allowed to decide—or rather whether the *majority* of inner-city residents alone should be allowed to decide. I do not think so. Instead of limiting the decision-making process to the inner city, we should invigorate wider public debate and encourage the courts to engage in and respond to our discussions. We should demand more transparent adjudication. We should encourage courts to set forth, more openly and fully, their conceptions of rights, in such a way as to allow for public debate, constructive criticism, and, possibly, judicial revision.

Unfortunately, Meares and Kahan ultimately fall back on a kind of formalism that may be counterproductive in this respect. The authors propose one legal presumption tied to one level of scrutiny. These kind of legal mechanisms frequently lead courts to sidestep full discussion of the issues. They become outcome-determinative. And they frequently silence public criticism. When a case is resolved on a technical legal ground, like a legal presumption or the level of scrutiny to be applied, it is difficult for non-lawyers to engage in the debate. In this regard, the Meares/Kahan proposal, again, is not democratic enough.

Why limit the political process and the resulting constitutional presumption to the communities that will be most immediately burdened? This is the only way, argue Meares and Kahan, to guarantee against oppression by the majority—against the risk that the majority of society won't bear the burdens of its laws but instead will abridge the liberty of a powerless or despised minority. But their solution—to empower the majority within a minority community—reminds me of a Russian *matrioshka* doll. When you open that doll, you find another: at each level of the majority/minority issue, we are faced with the same problem—the risk that the majority (now of the minority community) won't bear the burdens of its laws but instead will infringe upon the liberty of a powerless or despised minority within it.

In the end, there may not be a stable, faultless, and unchanging guarantee against the oppression of a minority or of a smaller minority within it. This is, after all, the principal insight of the refreshing way Meares and Kahan talk about rights: rights should be conceptualized in relation to the present social, economic, and political conditions in order to achieve the objective of avoiding majoritarian oppression. This significant insight moves us two steps forward. But rather than devolving the responsibility for balancing individual rights against the maintenance of public safety to the inner city, we should encourage more widespread public debate and more transparent judicial decision making. And, ultimately, if conditions become unacceptably oppressive, we will have to march in the streets again—and pray for another William O. Douglas.

Faith, Hope, and Charity

ANTHONY PAUL FARLEY

The 1960s were a time of storm and stress. They were also a time of faith, hope, and charity. They were a time when we bequeathed the future—in the form of respect for the least among us—to the best part of ourselves. As a child I was told that "the first shall be last and the last shall be first," and the 1960s saw a massive effort to put this vision into practice. We cannot reject the values of the 1960s without rejecting our best selves. We cannot put these values away like childish things.

Franz Fanon's philosophical writings became the bible for the anti-colonial movements of the era. Fanon pointed out the connection between colonial oppression and mental disorders: the "system" produces the very disorders it requires for its own justification. Fanon taught us that under colonialism each "native" internalizes the system's scorn and learns to strike at his own hated self-image in the mirror of his neighbor.

In the 1990s, the "War on Drugs" and its anti-loitering and curfew laws are a case in point. Dealing addictive, unhealthful drugs in one's own neighborhood is one of the myriad forms of collective autodestruction that keep the colonized in thrall. Continuing the war of all-against-all in the form of suspended rights is not, in and of itself, a solution to the problem. Rather it is the other side of the same problem. Things fall apart. In such times, the worst among us are filled with a passionate intensity.

Every twenty seconds someone in the United States is arrested for a drug violation. Every week, on average, a new prison is built. We possess the world's largest prison system, and blacks are now an absolute majority of prison inmates. No greater monument to anti-democracy can be imagined. And yet our imaginations are filled with a Manichean delirium. We imagine that the good and the bad can be separated, one from another and once and for all, if only we spend billions more on prisons. And prisons only foster recidivism.

Marching to the system's endless hymn of self-praise will not "win" the War on Drugs. It will merely serve to estrange us more deeply and profoundly from ourselves. The War on Drugs is the most hallucinogenic war of all time. Those who *enforce* the system's anti-drug procla-mations and those who *violate* them march in step. Illegal drug trafficking and use undermines communi-ties. The enforcement of anti–drug trafficking laws also undermines communities. Soldiers are soldiers. Vic-tims cannot distinguish between professional soldiers, citizen-soldiers, mercenaries, and bandits. The spiral of violence relies upon both lawmakers and lawbreakers.

Enshrining a local public-housing elite with a bit of state power will hardly pave a path to an emancipated future. Given the terrible conditions foisted upon blacks by our white-over-black government it is likely that we blacks, like prisoners everywhere, will agree to become the instruments of our own unmaking—that we will agree to any of the various Faustian bargains directed our way by our masters. And it is likely that by so doing we will kill the very best part of ourselves.

Blacks are still excluded from the nation's political life. Indeed, the U.S. Senate has not a single black member. Nor does it have a single member beholden to a majority-black constituency. And even those few blacks who have attained political office since the 1960s are rarely from, or responsible to, the black masses. A black drug warrior, like a white drug warrior, is a drug warrior. The Drug War is a tragic war on blacks, and increasing black representation among the drug warriors will not bring about a lasting peace.

Tragically, though, Tracey Meares and Dan Kahan are not completely wrong. Tragically, in our time, as in all times, something must be done. But what? Meares and Kahan suggest that we do something to give local people some form of democratic control over their own lives by allowing them to let go of certain rights much fetishized by those who do not live on the front lines of the War on Drugs. I agree. I also agree that "real-world experience belies the idea that spiraling inner-city crime will somehow force powerful interests *outside* the inner city to revitalize those communities." But democracy, radical democracy, may revitalize our communities.

If we accept building searches, curfews, anti-loitering ordinances, and the like, we must do this only as part of an overall strategy of radical democracy in which we end the War on Drugs and begin again the War on Poverty. In this way we can build a beloved community worthy of our aspirations. And to aspire for something better is, of course, to see the future so beautifully dreamed of during the revolutions of the 1960s.

Let us set open the prisons and release all of those who have been placed there for drug crimes not involving violence or large amounts of money, and declare peace by decriminalizing the offenses that caused their imprisonment. Let us beat our swords into ploughshares. We can redeploy the many billions of dollars that will thereby be saved to rebuild the infrastructure of our inner cities, to fund schools that will educate, to pay for healthful recreational activities for young and old alike. We can remember that the prisoner and the guard are linked by the same chains. We can break the chain and recover our souls in the process. And perhaps faith, hope, and charity can replace the desperate equations of the status quo.

The New Progressives

RICHARD H. PILDES

*I*n "Mechanical Jurisprudence," a classic essay in American legal scholarship, sociologist of law Roscoe Pound observed that American law oscillates between formalist and realist styles. When judges openly acknowledge the constant fluidity of society, they self-consciously attune legal rules to the realistic social consequences they think most likely to follow. But as any such body of legal principles matures, Pound wrote, it exhibits an almost inevitable tendency toward "petrifaction." Judges lose hold of the purposes that the legal principles were first designed to serve. Legal decisions become self-referential, a technical matter of applying rules "correctly" from the internal vantage point of the legal system itself. "Conceptions are fixed. Everything is reduced to simple deduction from them. Principles cease to have importance. The law becomes a body of rules." Thus is formalist, or mechanical, jurisprudence born.

To Tracey Meares and Dan Kahan, the admirable constitutional progressivism of the Warren Court is in danger of becoming just such a formalized, abstracted, mechanical body of rules. The constitutionalism of the

1960s was built on at least three central premises concerning the structure of solutions to problems of racial exclusion and oppression. First, strong assertions of national power were required. All national institutions were enlisted: the Supreme Court developed nationally binding constitutional rights; Congress enacted transformative statutes like the 1964 Civil Rights Act and the 1965 Voting Rights Act, and debated the issues and remedies at the national level; and the executive branch sent federal officials southward to register black voters and federal troops to supervise the integration of schools. The architects of these solutions also placed their faith in the potential of formal laws, like the Civil Rights Act and the Voting Rights Act. And they recognized that the problem of race was how to bring African-Americans into the full rights of citizenship after nearly a century of segregation and of virtually total disenfranchisement in the South.

Meares and Kahan's critique of rights is best seen as only one dimension of a more full-fronted challenge to all three premises. This broader challenge is increasingly characteristic of the current generation of constitutional progressives. While national institutions remain important, a chastened perspective has emerged on the likelihood that enduring change can emanate from such sources alone. Thus, Meares and Kahan are focused on local governments, or even more decentralized sources of decision making like public housing tenant councils, as today's venues for effective social change.

The limits of formal law have also become more apparent, and there is an emerging appreciation of the way formal law must interact with culture and social norms if it is to be effective. Whether or not one agrees with the specifics of Chicago's loitering ordinance, its most significant feature is the philosophy behind it: rather than trying to deter crime with aggressive sentencing after the fact, its framers seek to use law to influence the norms that govern public spaces. Less harsh police interventions, in advance of serious crime, are designed to help law-abiding citizens reclaim these spaces; and as the critical mass shifts, the presence of such citizens, it is hoped, will generate further norms that then make it more likely that these spaces will be put to good use. Finally, Meares and Kahan suggest that an ahistoric historicism characterizes some current writing on race and public policy—a narrative in which today's problems of race, while certainly real, are too often understood as just one more stage in a long-familiar struggle.

These analyses of the strengths and limits of 1960s constitutionalism are admittedly tentative, and the policy directions they suggest are undoubtedly provisional. For all the force of their writing, that is also the way in which I would take Meares and Kahan's arguments on the relationship between democracy and rights. I would not construe these as proposals for formal rules of constitutional law—that whenever the burdens of particular policies on rights are equally shared within the relevant "community" that has endorsed those policies, courts ought to accept them. Transformed into a formal rule of constitutional law, such an approach would confront the courts with profound conceptual questions, albeit ones that to some extent courts answer in other areas of law. What defines the relevant community? What does it mean for burdens to be equally shared?

Instead, I would see Meares and Kahan as arguing for a shift in attitudes that judges, civil libertarians, academics, activists, and others should bring to the kind of decentralized, participatory experiments now being tried to address vexing problems in cities, schools, and local institutions. Rather than casting these as yet another turn in a numbingly familiar morality play about state, race, and law (we know the good and bad actors in advance, and the script remains the same), Meares and Kahan ask for a less mechanical jurisprudence. Judges should once again become realists about social and political conditions, as many of the best once were on these topics. Judges should struggle to come to terms with the political contexts in which new, admittedly experimental approaches are being developed; those who do not live with the consequences of failed policies should do their best to grasp the social context in which these problems now arise, and evaluate new, locally adopted philosophies for dealing with them in light of the realistic alternatives. And because, as Tocqueville famously observed, the benefits of democratic participation lie not so much with the substantive decisions reached but with the energy, optimism, and spirit that participation as such unleashes in other spheres, we should certainly consider it a cost—perhaps appropriate at times, but a genuine cost—when communities are denied the power to come to their own judgments about what burdens they find worth bearing.

When Judge Anderson forbade the random sweeps of public housing projects that many tenants appear to have endorsed, he rehearsed a familiar shibboleth: the erosion of the rights of people on the other side of town will ultimately undermine the rights of each of us. Meares and Kahan want judges drawn to this heroic self-image—the protective defender of the despised outcast against the omnipotent state—to think again about what it means to embrace such an identity in today's context of local decision making. Similarly, when academics criticize initiatives like Chicago's loitering ordinance by hearkening back to 1693 legal edicts authorizing constables to seize any black person walking about without a pass from their master, as two University of Chicago law professors recently did,[1] Meares and Kahan are surely right: this ahistorical attitude toward history can only stand in the way of progress on the difficult issues of democracy, rights, and crime that trouble us today.

III

Reply

TRACEY L. MEARES AND DAN M. KAHAN

*R*ights don't determine their own content. Some institution—meaning some *person*—must decide whether inner-city curfews, gang-loitering laws, and building searches unreasonably subordinate liberty to order. So who should be empowered to make that moral judgment? Who has the experience, the values, and the stake in the outcome that qualify them to judge?

Our answer is that the residents of the inner-city themselves do. They are the ones who face the deadly risks associated with gang criminality.[1] But, equally important, they are the very individuals whose apartments are subject to emergency searches and whose sons and daughters, neighbors, and friends are subject to curfews and anti-loitering laws. Because these citizens are reasonable people, because they have every incentive to consider *all* the relevant interests, and because in the end it is *their* safety and freedom that is on the line, there's no reason to think that anyone else—whether professional civil libertarians, academic philosophers, or politically insulated judges—is in a better position to decide whether these policies strike a reasonable balance between liberty and order.

That was the heart of our essay. Many of the criticisms of it seem to be founded on misunderstanding, but at least some of the commentators' objections strike us as profound and important, and well worth the attention of anyone who is interested in how the law should take the political dynamics now reshaping inner-city policing into account. We address here the points upon which the commentators lay their primary emphasis.[2]

MAJORITARIANISM VERSUS RIGHTS

Several commentators accuse of us of ignoring the countermajoritarian logic of rights. Thus, Alan Dershowitz upbraids us for advancing "the proposition—rejected by all rights theories—that a majority can consent for an unwilling minority." Carol Steiker lectures us about the dangers of allowing "strong majoritarian sentiment to prevail" over "*constitutional* freedoms."

These criticisms rest on confusion. Of course, majorities can't override minority rights: that's what it means for an entitlement to be a *right*. But whether there *is* a right against housing searches, curfews, or gangloitering laws is exactly the issue here. In answering that question, the effect of these policies on the majority is plainly relevant: because they burden the majority as well

as the minority, it doesn't make sense to view these policies as reflecting the disregard for minority liberties that
rights are meant to prohibit.[3]

This theory of rights is in fact well established in the
American constitutional tradition. In its interpretation
of a diverse array of constitutional provisions—from
the Free Exercise Clause to the Free Speech Clause to the
Equal Protection Clause to the Takings Clause—the
Supreme Court has recognized that there is less need for
setting into motion the elaborate judicial institution of
rights, with all that entails, when majorities are sharing
in the burdens that they are imposing on minorities.
For example, in recent right-to-die cases, the Court ac-
knowledged that there are important questions of liberty
at stake, but it refused to constitutionalize the issue, in
part because the terminally ill were not a group against
whom democratic majorities should be thought to be bi-
ased or indifferent—which is precisely the kind of argument we are making here. Metal detectors in airports
and sobriety checkpoints on highways likewise burden
the liberty of the majority as well as the minority and
thus raise no issue of constitutional rights. Our argument is that the changing politics of inner-city law
enforcement—which Wesley Skogan describes in his
response[4]—now make it thinkable to apply this same
mode of analysis to various inner-city policing strategies
that impose significant burdens on the community at
large.

WHOSE COMMUNITY? WHOSE BURDENS?

Richard Pildes and Alan Dershowitz wonder how to determine whether the burden associated with a law or a practice—even one that applies on its face to all citizens—is really being "shared" by the community at large. This is an important and difficult issue that goes to the center of our argument. Dershowitz is surely right that no court should accept the claim that a largely Christian community is sharing in the burden associated with mandatory Christian prayer, since the members of that community wouldn't necessarily see the requirement as burdensome and couldn't be assumed to care about the sensibilities of the non-Christians who do. But if that's so, why say that the majority of the residents of Chicago Housing Authority projects are "really" sharing in the burden of emergency building searches when *they* don't experience those searches as being nearly so burdensome as does the minority of residents who oppose them?

This critique shows that the burden-sharing test turns as much on normative criteria as on factual ones. We can say that a political community is genuinely sharing in the burden associated with a particular policy only if we think that the average member of that community is affected by the policy in a way that entitles his or her appraisal of it to moral respect. The average member of a predominantly Christian community isn't affected in that way by a mandatory Christian prayer, given the negligible impact of that policy on her, and her indifference to its impact on her non-Christian neighbors. But the average resident of the inner city is affected that way, in our opinion, by building searches, curfews, and anti-loitering laws, given the *real* impact of those polices on her and her *affinity* to her children and her neighbors.

But how do we know that? In the end, there's no algorithm or abstract theory that can be used to determine whether the average citizen is affected in a way that warrants deference to his or her appraisal of the right balance of liberty and order. All one can do is decide, based on a vivid and rich reconstruction of that actor's circumstances, whether one has confidence in that citizen's judgment.

Again, there is no perspective-free vantage point for assessing what rights citizens have. Those who say that the average inner-city resident is *not* in a position to assess whether particular policing strategies impose an acceptable burden on liberty are necessarily saying that judges and civil libertarians—who represent the perspectives of even more remote and less meaningfully affected communities—*are*. We think anyone who listens to project resident Alverta Munlyn's explanation of why she supports building searches, to Dallas mother Edna Pemberton's defense of youth curfews, or to the testimony of South Side residents in favor of Chicago's gang-loitering law will come away with immense respect for their local knowledge. We challenge anyone who has read Judge Anderson's opinion in the CHA case, or who has heard civil libertarians explain why they side with the suburbanites who opposed inner-city curfews in Washington, D.C., Dallas, and San Diego, to explain why we should respect their perspective more.

BUT IS IT GOOD FOR THE BLACKS?

We draw fire from all sides on the question of whether our position conduces to the well-being of African-Americans. Dershowitz, for example, ridicules us for presenting an "Afrocentric" account of rights, while Steiker contends that the policies we defend are inimical to the interests of African-Americans and, in the case of the gang-loitering law, are actually opposed by most of them. Other commentators chide us for implying that African-Americans speak with a "single voice."

This collection of arguments reflects more confusion. We do not propose to decide whether a policing strategy violates rights by considering how it affects the welfare of African-Americans. The standard we *do* use is whether the coercive burden of the policy is being visited on a powerless minority or is instead being shared in by the larger community. We emphasize the significant support of minority inner-city residents for gang-loitering laws, curfews, and building searches to show that these policies, unlike an earlier generation of public order laws, are not aimed at reinforcing the exclusion of minorities from the nation's political and economic life.

Steiker disputes this, but her account of the politics behind the Chicago gang-loitering law is flawed. As recently as May 1998, a majority of African-American alderman voted in favor of the ordinance. Likewise, when the Chicago City Council initially voted in 1992, the ordinance would have been defeated by a wide margin rather than passed by one had it not had the support of aldermen representing twelve of the city's highest-crime minority neighborhoods.[5]

None of this is to say (nor did we ever say) that African-Americans speak with a "single voice" on any of these issues. Of course there are differences of opinion among African-Americans—as there are among whites, Latinos, and every other group of citizens—about whether such policies are a good idea. But the very fact that such disagreement is now occurring within and across ethnic and racial communities, and not simply between them—the very fact that these policies raise issues that are vexingly gray, and not starkly black-and-white—underscores how dramatically the political context has changed since the Supreme Court fashioned the 1960s conception of rights. That's all our 1990s conception presupposes.

DEFORMED PREFERENCES

Alan Dershowitz purports "never" to have "heard a genuine civil libertarian make the absurd and demeaning paternalist argument attributed to us by Meares and Kahan." He'll be edified, then, when he reads the critiques of his fellow commentators. From Joel Handler he'll learn what "scholars and activists working with dependent people have known for a long time," namely, that the expressed preferences of *these* people are not a reliable measure of what they "really want." From Carol Steiker he'll learn that the support of inner-city communities for curfews, gang-loitering laws, and building searches should be disregarded because the choices they face are too "hard" for them to make for themselves. Are we really supposed to believe that the cartoonish hypotheticals served up to first-year law school students teach us anything about the competence of inner-city residents to make up their own minds? These are the exactly the sorts of rhetorical moves that Jean Elshtain has in mind when she complains of "liberal condescension."

SHIFTING PREFERENCES

Bernard Harcourt, in contrast, suggests a variant of the "deformed preferences" argument that deserves to be taken seriously. He doesn't attack the competence of inner-city residents to decide for themselves right now whether the impact of building searches, curfews, and gang-loitering laws exact an unreasonable toll on their liberty. But he does worry about the effect such policies might have in enervating citizens' resistance toward invasive policies in the *future*. "We are all shaped by the policing practices that we, as a society, condone, witness, experience, and inflict," he writes.

Interestingly, Harcourt has an improbable ally in this argument: Justice Antonin Scalia. Expressing skepticism that "the fiercely proud men who adopted our Fourth Amendment would have allowed themselves to be subjected" to the "indignity" of protective stop-and-frisks, Scalia has taken the position that the Fourth Amendment should be read to lock in the framers' intolerance of invasive policing "even if a later, less virtuous age should become accustomed to considering all sorts of intrusion 'reasonable.'"[6] On this account, rights don't embody the obligation of the state to respect individuals' own preferences; instead, they are an instrument for sustaining the supposedly ideal dispositions of the framers.

We don't view the position taken by Harcourt and Scalia as a reason to back off from our initial arguments. Their anxiety that policing techniques that are admittedly "reasonable"—such as curfews, gang-loitering laws, and building searches—might nevertheless erode our society's "virtuous" resentment of state authority is speculative. We can't disprove it. But only someone who is complacent about the status quo would treat such speculation as sufficient grounds to abort experimentation with milder public order alternatives to the crackdown policies that dominate law enforcement today.

MORE DEMOCRACY?

Anthony Paul Farley also worries about the civic capacities of inner-city residents, and concludes that curfews, gang-loitering laws, and building searches should be on the agenda "only as part of an overall strategy of radical democracy in which we end the War on Drugs and begin again the War on Poverty." We agree with him that *more* democracy rather than *less* is the best way to assure that citizens in the inner-city, and elsewhere, develop the dispositions upon which democratic citizenship depends. We hope that he and others who see things his way understand, though, that denying these communities the opportunity to approve the policies we've defended makes revitalized democracy less likely, not more, by stripping community activists of a critical focal point for mobilizing local residents.

Conceptions of rights have life cycles. They are born of practical need, flourish in an atmosphere of general utility, and decline as changing conditions drain them of their vitality. When the contradiction between a view of rights and social necessity finally becomes too intense to be endured, that conception expires—sometimes peacefully, sometimes convulsively—and is superseded by another one that is fated to enjoy the same career.

The 1960s conception of rights has outlived its utility. It is now time to construct a *new* conception, one uniquely fitted to the conditions that currently characterize American social and political life and are likely to characterize it into the foreseeable future.

Notes

Tracey L. Meares and Dan M. Kahan / *When Rights Are Wrong*

1. Each CHA development has a Local Advisory Council (LAC), the members of which are elected by that development's residents. The presidents of each LAC serve on a Central Advisory Council, which adopted a resolution officially approving the building search policy and authorizing LAC presidents to intervene against the ACLU lawsuit.

2. The Supreme Court's equal protection jurisprudence explicitly reflects the idea that courts should prevent majorities from singling out politically powerless minorities for special burdens (see John Hart Ely, *Democracy and Distrust* [Cambridge, Mass.: Harvard University Press, 1980]). But the same idea *implicitly* animated much of the rest of the Warren Court's expansive jurisprudence of constitutional rights. The Court, of course, played a conspicuous role in the movement to purge American institutions of the contaminating influence of racism in the 1950s and 1960s. The Court's leading race-equality cases, including *Brown v. Board of Education*, 347 U.S. 483 (1954), and the apportionment case of *Baker v. Carr*, 369 U.S. 186 (1962), provoked intense political controversy. Confronted with a sustained attack on its own legitimacy, the Court changed its tactics. Rather than meet racism head on, the Court began to fight it indirectly through general constitutional standards that did not explicitly address race but that were nonetheless calculated to constrain racially motivated policies. Harry Kalven, in his classic *The Negro and the First Amendment* (Chicago: University of Chicago Press, 1965), documented the contribution that this strategy made to modern free speech jurisprudence. The Court's death penalty jurisprudence in the late 1960s and early 1970s likewise reflected a (largely) unspoken

concern with race. See Carol S. Steiker and Jordan M. Steiker, "Sober Second Thoughts: Reflections on Two Decades of Constitutional Regulation of Capital Punishment," *Harvard Law Review* 109 (1995).

3. Randall Kennedy, *Race, Crime, and the Law* (Cambridge, Mass.: Harvard University Press, 1997).

4. See *Chicago v. Morales*, 119 S. Ct. 1849 (1999).

CAROL S. STEIKER / *More Wrong Than Rights*

1. See *Williams v. Walker-Thomas Furniture Co.*, 350 F.2d 445 (D.C. Cir. 1965).

2. See *Official Journal*, City of Chicago, p. 18,293 (17 June 1992). Eight African-American aldermen voted against the ordinance, and four did not vote. Those opposed to the ordinance spoke in vehement terms against the racial consequences of such legislation, comparing the ordinance to South Africa's now-defunct pass laws and to Hitler's policies oppressing Jews in Germany.

3. The Fourth Amendment promises, "The right of the people to be secure in their persons, houses, papers, and effects, against unreasonable searches and seizures, shall not be violated."

4. See *Brinegar v. United States*, 338 U.S. 160, 180–81 (1949) (Jackson, J., dissenting).

5. See *Skinner v. Railway Labor Executives' Association*, 489 U.S. 602, 635 (1989) (Marshall, J., dissenting).

MARGARET A. BURNHAM / *Twice Victimized*

1. Memorandum from Justice William J. Brennan to Chief Justice Earl Warren on *Terry v. Ohio*, 14 March 1968, Papers of Chief Justice Earl Warren, Manuscript Room, Library of Congress, Washington, D.C.

FRANKLIN E. ZIMRING / *A Multi-Problem Theory*

1. Compare U.S. Department of Justice, *Uniform Crime Report*, for the years 1986 and 1996.

Notes

Bernard E. Harcourt / *Matrioshka Dolls*

1. Cornel West, *Race Matters* (Boston: Beacon Press, 1993), 21.

2. In a recent article, I sketched out what an assessment might look like for one specific police practice: New York City's strategy of aggressive misdemeanor arrests for minor disorderly conduct. See Bernard E. Harcourt, "Reflecting on the Subject: A Critique of the Social Influence Conception of Deterrence, the Broken Windows Theory, and Order-Maintenance Policing New York Style," *Michigan Law Review* 97 (1998): 291–389.

Richard H. Pildes / *The New Progressives*

1. Albert Alschuler and Stephen Schulhofer, "Antiquated Procedures or Bedrock Rights?: A Response to Professors Meares and Kahan," *University of Chicago Legal Forum* 215 (1998): 243.

Tracey L. Meares and Dan M. Kahan / *Reply*

1. Zimring notes that the homicide rate for African-Americans has declined in the 1990s. This is true in aggregate, but the declines are unevenly distributed. See Pamela K. Lattimore et al., *Homicide in Eight U.S. Cities: Trends, Context, and Policy Implications* 1 (U.S. Dept. of Justice, December 1997). Indeed, many urban centers—from Atlanta to Detroit to Miami to Indianapolis to New Orleans—have seen increases in homicide for young African-American men during this period. See ibid., 33. In many cities where violent crime has declined—including New York and Boston—order-maintenance policing strategies similar to the ones we are defending deserve at least part of the credit. See Tracey L. Meares and Dan M. Kahan, "Law and (Norms of) Order in the Inner-City," *Law & Society Review* (forthcoming 1999). In any case, it would be ludicrous to dispute that our nation's predominantly minority inner-city neighborhoods remain dangerous places to live, both in comparison to other communities and in absolute terms.

2. We discuss these and other arguments in greater detail in

Dan M. Kahan and Tracey L. Meares, "The Coming Crisis of Criminal Procedure," *Georgetown Law Journal* 86 (1998): 1153.

3. Margaret Burnham plainly misreads our argument. We aren't proposing "the idea that insular poor black communities . . . be allowed to opt out of constitutional rules"; our position is that the burden of these policies on the majority's own liberty is a reason to conclude that such policies don't impose an unconstitutional diminution of liberty. Jeremy Waldron is likewise missing the point when he criticizes us for ignoring the difference between "waivers" and "abandonments" of rights. Because these policies, in our view, don't *violate* rights, the question of whether inner-city residents are waiving or instead abandoning them doesn't arise.

4. And which he and Susan Hartnett address in even greater detail in their book *Community Policing, Chicago Style* (New York: Oxford University Press, 1997).

5. See generally Tracey L. Meares and Dan M. Kahan, "Black, White, and Gray: A Reply to Alschuler and Schulhofer," *University of Chicago Legal Forum* 245 (1998): 246–51.

6. *Minnesota v. Dickerson*, 508 U.S. 366, 380–82 (1993) (Scalia, J., concurring).

ABOUT THE CONTRIBUTORS

MARGARET A. BURNHAM is a civil rights attorney. She teaches political science at MIT.

ALAN M. DERSHOWITZ is Felix Frankfurter Professor of Law at Harvard Law School. His most recent book is *Sexual McCarthyism: Clinton, Starr, and the Emerging Constitutional Crisis.*

JEAN BETHKE ELSHTAIN is Laura Spelman Rockefeller Professor of Social and Political Ethics at the University of Chicago. She is the author of *Democracy on Trial* and many other works.

ANTHONY PAUL FARLEY, a former prosecutor with the Office of the United States Attorney for the District of Columbia, is assistant professor of law at Boston College.

JOEL F. HANDLER teaches law at UCLA.

BERNARD E. HARCOURT is associate professor at the University of Arizona College of Law.

DAN M. KAHAN, a former law clerk to Justice Thurgood Marshall, is professor of law at the University of Chicago Law School.

TRACEY L. MEARES is assistant professor of law at the University of Chicago Law School.

RICHARD H. PILDES, a former law clerk to Justice Thurgood Marshall, is professor of law at the University of Michigan Law School.

WESLEY G. SKOGAN is a professor of political science and a faculty fellow of the Institute for Policy Research at Northwestern University. He is writing a book about community policing in Chicago.

CAROL S. STEIKER, professor of law and associate dean for academic affairs at Harvard Law School, served as a law clerk to Judge J. Skelly Wright of the D.C. Circuit Court of Appeals and to Justice Thurgood Marshall of the United States Supreme Court.

JEREMY WALDRON is Maurice and Hilda Friedman Professor of Law and director of the Center for Law and Philosophy at Columbia University.

FRANKLIN E. ZIMRING is William Simon Professor of Law and director of the Earl Warren Legal Institute at the University of California at Berkeley. His most recent book is *American Youth Violence*.

Printed in the United States
By Bookmasters